3-D EARTH

LONDON, NEW YORK,
MELBOURNE, MUNICH, AND
DELHI

DK LONDON
Senior Editor Niki Foreman
Senior Art Editor Sheila Collins
Editor Matilda Gollon
Augmented Reality Development
Steven Carton
Managing Editor Linda Esposito
Managing Art Editor
Diane Peyton Jones
Category Publisher Laura Buller

Publishing Director Jonathan Metcalf
Associate Publishing Director
Liz Wheeler
Art Director Phil Ormerod

Production Controller Angela Graef
Production Editor Joanna Byrne
DK Picture Library Emma Shepherd,
Rose Horridge
Picture Research Nic Dean
Design Development Manager
Sophia M. Tampakopoulos
Jacket Editor Manisha Majithia
Jacket Designer Laura Brim

AUGMENTED BY
TOTAL IMMERSION ▲◀

3-D Digital Artist Arran Lewis
For Pure Digital:
Director and Animation
Rob Cook
Director and Programming
Paul Hetherington

DK DELHI
Managing Art Editor
Arunesh Talapatra
Senior Art Editor Balwant Singh
Art Editor Anjana Nair
Assistant Designers Neha Sharma,
Payal Rosalind Malik, Nidhi Mehra
Deputy Managing Editor
Pakshalika Jayaprakash
Senior Editor Garima Sharma
Editor Pragati Nagpal
Production Manager Pankaj Sharma
DTP Manager Balwant Singh
DTP Designers Nand Kishor Acharya,
Tanveer Zaidi

First published in the United States in 2012
by DK Publishing
375 Hudson Street
New York, New York 10014

A catalog record for this book
is available from the Library of Congress.

ISBN 978-0-7566-9020-5

Hi-res workflow proofed by MDP, UK
Printed and bound in China by Hung Hing

Discover more at
www.dk.com

3-D
EARTH

Written by
John Woodward

Consultant
Kim Bryan

DK

Contents

06 Planet Earth

08 Solar System

10 Planet formation

12 Core, mantle, and crust

14 Water world

16 Dynamic Earth

18 Mobile plates

20 Oceans and continents

22 Rifts and trenches

24 Earthquakes and tsunamis

26 Building mountains

28 Volcanoes and geysers

HOW TO INSTALL THE SOFTWARE

1 Download the software from www.3Dpops.dkonline.com and follow the on-screen instructions to install the software on your computer.

2 In the book there are six Augmented Reality (AR) spreads. Look for the blue logo in the right-hand corner of the page.

3 Sit in front of the computer with the book in front of you and your webcam turned on, and make sure your book is in view of the webcam.

Volcanoes and geyse

Volcanic eruptions are the most dramatic of all geological events. Searingly hot molten rock flows downhill in rivers of fire, and vast clouds billow into the sky to block the Sun. Some volcanoes erupt often, so they are predictable. But others may lie dormant for centuries, then suddenly explode and produce avalanches of hot gas and rock that can wipe out entire cities.

Show the main image to your webcam to start the AR animation.

LETHAL MIX
The most dangerous volcanoes erupt from plate boundaries where one plate is pushing beneath another, carrying sea-floor sediments and water down into the mantle. The water lowers the melting point of the mantle rock, so it melts and erupts from volcanoes. The meltwater makes the lava more viscous so it does not flow easily and also sets off gas, a deadly combination that causes violent, explosive eruptions.

30 Minerals & rocks

32 Minerals

34 Rocks

36 Fossils

38 The rock cycle

40 Caves

42 Weather & climate

44 Climate zones

46 Wind and rain

48 Extreme weather

50 Rivers, lakes, and wetlands

52 Snow, glaciers, and ice sheets

54 Changing climates

56 Life

58 Origins of life

60 Aquatic life

62 Forests

64 Grasslands

66 Deserts

68 Glossary

70 Index

72 Credits

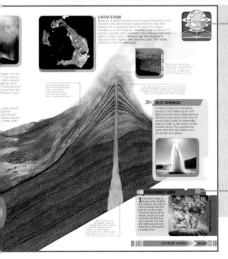

CATACLYSM
Eruptions of island volcanoes can be hugely destructive. Such eruptions form above broad magma chambers filled with molten rock. A massive eruption can empty the magma chamber, so its roof collapses. Seawater rushes into the roof void and explodes with cataclysmic force, blowing a vast cloud called a caldera. Some 3,600 years ago this happened to Santorini in the Aegean, seen here from space. The central caldera is 10 km (7.5 miles) long.

AR logo is in the right-hand corner of the AR spread.

HOT SPRINGS
If water touches hot rock below ground, it can bubble up as a hot spring. In some places high pressure allows it to get much hotter than its usual boiling point, but eventually some is forced to the surface as the pressure drops. The superheated water then boils and blasts out of the ground as a geyser.

Place your hand over each trigger box in turn to control the animations.

VOLCANIC ASH
If an active volcano is clogged with volcanic lava, pressure can build up until it explodes with the force of a nuclear bomb. This blasts the top of the volcano, forming a plume of debris and dust that rises high in the sky. But some may flood back and burst down as a high-speed pyroclastic flow.

DYNAMIC EARTH   28-29

4 Show the central image on the open page to the webcam and the AR animation will jump to life from the pages of your book and appear on your computer screen.

5 To see the next part of the animations, place your hand over one of the trigger boxes. Each trigger box is labeled with a hand symbol to show that it is a trigger box, and the boxes are numbered in the order that they should be covered.

Planet Earth

Our planet is one
of countless billions of
stars and planets in the
Universe. There could be others like
it, because the forces and elements
that created it are universal throughout
the vastness of space. But despite years of
searching, astronomers have not
discovered another planet with the same
dynamic geology, insulating oxygen-rich
atmosphere, and oceans of liquid water.
This is the combination that makes
planet Earth so unique, because it
supports its most important
feature—life.

Solar System

Earth is one of eight major planets orbiting the medium-sized star we call the Sun, to form the Solar System. It is part of the Milky Way galaxy, one of many galaxies in the Universe, each containing billions of stars and planets. This vast quantity of matter was created by nuclear fusion within giant stars— a process that turns light elements such as gases into heavier ones. These elements form our planet, and everything on it.

STARS AND GALAXIES

The Universe is made up of at least 100 billion galaxies. Each is a spinning, disk-shaped mass of stars, and each star has its own orbiting planets, asteroids, and comets. The stars are basically hot gas, while their planets are made of gases, liquids, and solid rock. There are also vast clouds of space dust, as well as mysterious dark matter that we cannot see.

THE SUN

The Sun is a huge ball of hot gas roughly 109 times the width of Earth. It formed around 4.6 billion years ago from a spinning cloud of dust and gas. Around three-quarters of its mass is hydrogen, the lightest of all gases; the rest is mostly helium, which is the next lightest. Despite this, the Sun accounts for 99 percent of the mass of the Solar System.

Mercury

Mars

Venus

Earth

Jupiter

Satur

NUCLEAR FURNACES

A star expands over time and some explode as a supernova like this one. In the process, it generates enough energy to fuse atoms together to make new elements. Our Sun fuses hydrogen to make helium. Bigger stars fuse helium to create carbon, fuse helium with carbon to form oxygen, and so on. Supernovas create the heaviest elements of all, such as metals.

NUCLEAR FUSION

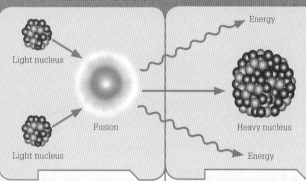

Light nucleus

Fusion

Light nucleus

Energy

Heavy nucleus

Energy

Fusing nuclei
All matter is made of atoms. An atom has a nucleus made of protons and neutrons. Nuclear fusion welds two nuclei together to make a heavier nucleus.

New element
A heavier atomic nucleus contains more protons, and the number of protons defines the element. Thus, an iron nucleus has 26 protons; a heavier gold nucleus has 79.

Neptune

ELEMENTS AND COMPOUNDS

Nuclear fusion in the stars has created all 94 elements that exist naturally on Earth, from hydrogen (the lightest) to plutonium (the heaviest). Some elements such as gold occur in pure form, as in this gold nugget. But most elements combine to form chemical compounds such as water (a compound of hydrogen and oxygen) and rock salt (sodium and chlorine).

ORBITING PLANETS

When the Sun formed it was surrounded by a spinning disk of dust and gas made up of all the elements and various chemical compounds. Most of this material clumped together to form the orbiting planets of the Solar System. These consist of the four inner rocky planets, Mercury, Venus, Earth, and Mars; the two giant gas planets, Jupiter and Saturn; the two ice giants, Uranus and Neptune; and several dwarf planets.

VITAL ENERGY

Nuclear fusion in the core of the Sun releases vast amounts of energy, partly in the form of heat and light. The heat keeps Earth warm enough for water to exist as a liquid, which is critical for life. Plants use the light to make their own food via photosynthesis, and they are then eaten by animals. Thus, the energy radiated by the Sun is vital to the thing that makes Earth so special—life.

Planet formation

Earth and the other planets were created from a mass of rocky debris orbiting the Sun. Around 4.56 billion years ago some of this debris clumped together to form a rocky sphere, or protoplanet. Over time this process generated so much heat that the early Earth melted, creating its layered internal structure before it started to cool and solidify. When the Earth collided with another similar planet, the impact resulted in the creation of the Moon.

RAW MATERIALS

Many of the meteors that travel through the night sky are made of the material that originally formed Earth. Some are made of iron, while others are stony and contain other elements such as carbon. Many are pieces of planets that broke up long ago. Others are fragments of space rock, built up from elements orginally forged in the furnaces of giant stars.

ACCRETION

Objects floating in space attract each other by the force of gravity, so they smash together to form bigger objects. The bigger they get, the more gravity they have, and the more they attract each other in an accelerating process called accretion. Over many millions of years this turned an orbiting mass of small rock fragments into a rocky planet.

MELTDOWN

As the early Earth grew by accretion, all the impact energy was transformed into heat. This made the protoplanet hotter and hotter, until it eventually melted. Gravity then made the heavier elements such as iron sink toward the center of the molten sphere, leaving the lighter rocky elements nearer to the surface. The planet then cooled to create its layered structure of core, mantle, and crust.

COSMIC CRASH

Impact

Early Earth

Collision course
When Earth formed, its orbit around the Sun coincided with the orbit of another planet roughly the size of Mars. Approximately 4.5 billion years ago they slammed together in a catastrophic collision.

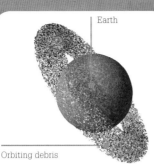

Earth

Orbiting debris

Debris cloud
The impact energy of the collision was converted into heat that partly melted Earth again, and completely destroyed the other planet. The fragments formed an orbiting ring of rocky debris around Earth.

Moon

Cooling Earth

New Moon
Over time, the accretion process that created Earth turned all the orbiting debris into the Moon. As with Earth, the process generated heat that melted the Moon and created a layered structure.

Every day hundreds of meteorites hit Earth and make it very slightly bigger, so the planet is still growing.

THE MOON
Analysis of rocks from the Moon shows that it is made of much the same material as Earth, but its metallic core is probably relatively small. Since the Moon is smaller than Earth, it has far less mass, so it does not have enough gravity to hold on to an insulating atmosphere. This means that its cratered surface is scalding hot by day and extremely cold at night.

COOLING EARTH
Once the Moon had formed, Earth began to cool again. Its interior stayed extremely hot, but the crust cooled so water vapor that had erupted from volcanoes condensed into clouds and rain. This poured down in a deluge that gradually flooded the planet with a vast global ocean. Meanwhile, nitrogen, carbon dioxide, and other gases formed an insulating atmosphere that kept most of the water liquid, permitting the evolution of life.

Core, mantle, and crust

Earth is a ball of hot rock with a dense metallic core and a thin, cool crust. Most of the interior is solid, despite its very high temperature, because the intense pressure at that depth stops it from melting. Where rifts in the crust ease the pressure, the hot rock melts and erupts as lava from volcanoes. These also erupt water vapor and other gases that add to the oceans and atmosphere.

METALLIC CORE

When Earth melted early in its history, a lot of the heavy metallic elements such as iron, nickel, and uranium sank to the center of the molten planet. Here, they eventually formed a solid inner core, surrounded by a liquid outer core of molten metal and some other elements. Together they form a ball of metal 4,350 miles (7,000 km) across, which is roughly the size of Mars. The huge mass of this metallic core gives Earth much of its gravity.

Earth's inner core is probably made of the same metals as this meteorite, which struck Siberia in Russia in 1947. It is 93 percent iron and 6 percent nickel, with the rest made up of phosphorus, cobalt, and sulfur. It probably came from the core of a shattered planet.

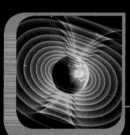

The molten metallic outer core is stirred up by heat currents. This generates electrical currents that create an electromagnetic field around the planet. The form of the field is always changing, so the magnetic north pole is shifting all the time.

The metallic core is surrounded by the mantle—a very deep layer of hot, solid, but slowly moving rock that makes up 84 percent of the planet. Much of the upper mantle is made of peridotite, the greenish material that forms most of this lump of volcanic rock.

The crust is the thin skin of the planet. The thinnest parts are the ocean floors, while the thickest form mountain ranges. Movement in the hot mantle beneath the brittle crust rips it apart to create rifts and faults like this one. It has also divided the crust into many separate plates.

We can see the top of the crust but we only know what lies beneath through the science of seismology. Scientists analyze the seismic waves that radiate from earthquakes and pass through the planet. The data they collect shows how the waves are obstructed and deflected by its internal structure, and this indicates the density, nature, and thickness of Earth's layers.

BLUE PLANET

Above the crust, two-thirds of the planet is covered by ocean water. We don't normally think of water as part of the planet's structure, but like rock it is a natural chemical compound, and it can be just as solid when it freezes to form ice. Most of the water probably erupted as water vapor from vast volcanoes early in the history of the planet, initially forming part of the atmosphere. Volcanoes still erupt a lot of water vapor today. However, some of the water in the oceans may have been delivered to Earth from outer space by comets crashing onto its surface, because comets are largely made of ice.

Atmospheric ozone shields us from lethal ultraviolet light—we could not survive without it.

VITAL ATMOSPHERE

The atmosphere forms a blanket of air that extends for about 435 miles (700 km) above the surface, gradually thinning out until it is virtually undetectable. It consists of 78 percent nitrogen and 21 percent oxygen, plus tiny amounts of other gases including carbon dioxide, water vapor, and ozone. It forms distinct layers, and four-fifths of its mass—including nearly all the water vapor—is concentrated in the lowest layer, the troposphere. The carbon dioxide and some other gases provide insulation that keeps the average global temperature 86°F (30°C) higher than it is on the airless Moon.

Water world

Seen from space, Earth is a blue planet, largely covered by oceans. But water is not unique to Earth. It is found throughout space, but mainly as ice or gaseous water vapor. Earth is unusual because its temperature allows water to exist as a solid, liquid, and gas, in the oceans and atmosphere. We owe this to the happy accident of Earth's orbital distance from the Sun, which lies in a region of space that is neither too hot nor too cold, but just right.

STICKY MOLECULES

Water is a mass of molecules, each formed from two hydrogen atoms and one oxygen atom. The atoms are held together by electric charges that make them form triangles. These triangular molecules act like tiny magnets, attracting each other so they stick together as liquid water.

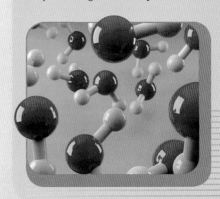

OTHER WORLDS

We know that there is water elsewhere in the Solar System, but very little of it is liquid. There is certainly water on Mars, but most of it is solid ice. Comets are largely made of ice mixed with rock fragments, and there is water on Mercury, but only in the form of water vapor. However, there is a possibility that Europa (left), one of the moons of Jupiter, has oceans of liquid saltwater beneath its gleaming surface of cracked ice.

Water is the only substance that gets less dense when it freezes. This is why ice floats.

SOLID, LIQUID, GAS

1 If water gets cold enough, its molecules lock together as solid ice. When the Sun melts the ice, the molecules unlock and start moving around as a flowing liquid. At any temperature above freezing, some break free and enter the air as water vapor, allowing water to exist in all three forms at once in the same place.

Oceans and seas contain 97 percent of the world's water. They are in constant motion, whipped up into waves by the winds and flowing in currents that eventually carry every drop of ocean water all around the globe.

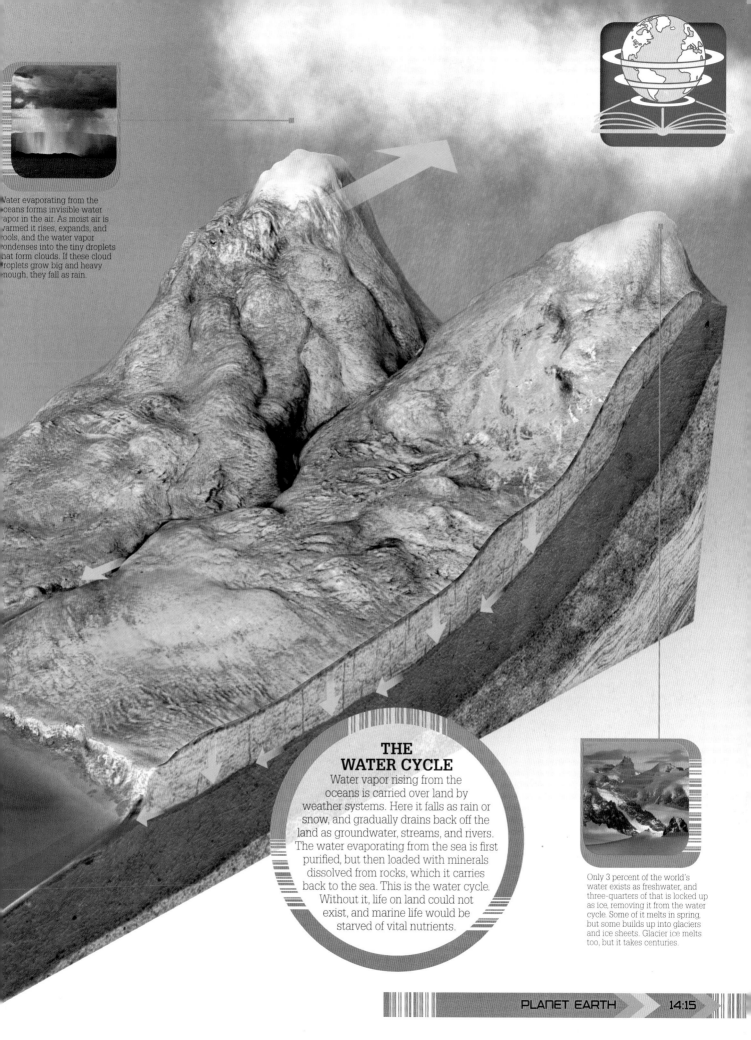

Water evaporating from the oceans forms invisible water vapor in the air. As moist air is warmed it rises, expands, and cools, and the water vapor condenses into the tiny droplets that form clouds. If these cloud droplets grow big and heavy enough, they fall as rain.

THE WATER CYCLE

Water vapor rising from the oceans is carried over land by weather systems. Here it falls as rain or snow, and gradually drains back off the land as groundwater, streams, and rivers. The water evaporating from the sea is first purified, but then loaded with minerals dissolved from rocks, which it carries back to the sea. This is the water cycle. Without it, life on land could not exist, and marine life would be starved of vital nutrients.

Only 3 percent of the world's water exists as freshwater, and three-quarters of that is locked up as ice, removing it from the water cycle. Some of it melts in spring, but some builds up into glaciers and ice sheets. Glacier ice melts too, but it takes centuries.

Dynamic Earth

Water spouts from
the Fly Geyser,
Nevada

If you look at the Moon in the night sky, you will see an inert lump of rock, pitted with ancient craters. Little has changed it in many millions of years. By contrast, Earth is being constantly remodeled by geological processes that rearrange its continents and trigger dramatic events such as earthquakes and volcanic eruptions. These processes have erased most of the evidence of Earth's early history, and have been vital to the evolution of life.

Mobile plates

Earth's crust is constantly moving, driven by heat currents that boil up from deep within the planet and flow through the solid but mobile rock of the mantle. The movement is extremely slow, but immensely powerful. It has ripped the cool, brittle crust into vast rocky plates that are pulling apart in some places and grinding together in others. It triggers earthquakes, fuels volcanoes, and builds mountains, and over millions of years it completely reshapes the global map.

DEEP HEAT

Ever since the cataclysmic event that formed the Moon, planet Earth has been cooling down. But the process has been slowed by the generation of heat deep within the planet's mantle and core. The source of this heat is the radioactive decay of very heavy elements such as uranium, which naturally form part of the rocks. This releases nuclear energy in the form of heat, which rises through the mantle toward the surface where it is radiated into space.

Radioactive decay is a slow process, so it can take many millions of years for half a radioactive element to decay into a lighter, stable form. This means that elements such as uranium have been generating energy throughout Earth's history.

RADIOACTIVE DECAY

The atoms of elements have nuclei made up of smaller particles called protons and neutrons. The atomic nuclei of very heavy elements, such as uranium, have hundreds of particles, and are so massive that they tend to fall apart. Particles are lost in a process called radioactive decay that also releases nuclear energy as heat. Over time this turns heavy elements into lighter, stable elements such as lead.

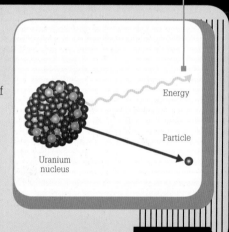

Uranium nucleus

Energy

Particle

BOILING UP

Although the rock of Earth's mantle is kept solid by intense pressure, it is extremely hot. This allows it to flow very slowly, driven by heat rising from deep inside the planet. Convection currents in the rock rise to beneath the crust and then flow sideways, dragging the crust with them. Where they diverge, they pull the crust apart, and where they sink back into the mantle, they carry some of the crust down with them.

Heat rising from near the core sets up convection currents in the mantle rock, in the same way as heat rising through a pot of simmering soup. The hot rock rises, cools, and sinks back toward the core, where it heats up again.

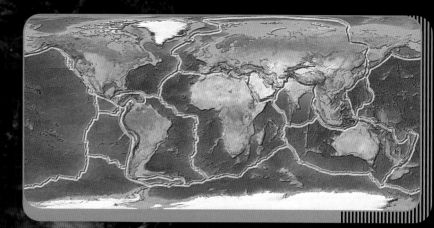

FRAGMENTED WORLD

The moving mantle has ripped the crust into seven major tectonic plates, seven minor plates, and up to 60 microplates. The biggest is the Pacific Plate that forms part of the Pacific Ocean floor, and covers 70 million sq miles (180 million sq km). Other major plates carry the continents of North America, South America, Africa, Eurasia, Australia, and Antarctica.

Until 45 million years ago, the Pacific Plate was slipping north, but then it began changing course and started heading northwest. This change is recorded as a kink in the line of volcanoes created by the plate moving over the mantle hot spot.

CREEPING CRUST

All the tectonic plates are creeping very slowly around the globe. The Pacific Plate is moving northwest at about 4 in (10 cm) a year, and over millions of years a stationary hot spot in the mantle beneath the moving plate has burned a chain of volcanoes that traces this movement. It extends across the ocean floor from Siberia to Hawaii, where volcanoes now over the hot spot are still active.

FRONTIER ZONES

The boundaries between tectonic plates are the danger zones of the world, because they are dotted with volcanoes and regularly shaken by earthquakes. The plate boundaries around the Pacific Plate are so violently active that they have formed a near-global chain of volcanoes and earthquake zones known as the "Pacific ring of fire." It extends all around the ocean from Alaska—the site of this massive earthquake in 1964—to New Zealand and back north to Japan, which were both struck much more recently.

Oceans and continents

The ocean floors are geologically different from the continents. They are made of a heavier, thinner, lower-lying type of crust that is similar to the mantle rock below. Continental crust is thicker and lighter, so the continents float on the dense mantle rock like icebergs in a polar ocean—and are carried slowly around the globe by the relentless forces of plate tectonics.

UNDERSEA VOLCANOES

All the bedrock of the ocean floors has erupted from undersea volcanoes as molten lava. When it touches the cold water the outside of the lava freezes. However the rock inside is still liquid, and the pressure makes it squirt out before hardening in turn. This creates a series of sausagelike lumps of rock known as pillow lavas, which form the ocean floors.

OCEAN FLOOR

Earth's upper mantle is made of a dark, heavy rock called peridotite. Although very hot, it is kept solid by intense pressure. But at the top of the upper mantle, lower pressure allows partial melting. This creates a lighter form of peridotite that cools to form a relatively thin layer of basalt—the bedrock of the ocean floors. In places this rock erupts from volcanoes to form spectacular rock formations, like these basalt columns on the Scottish island of Staffa.

CONTINENTAL DRIFT

The continents are rooted in the mobile plates of the Earth's crust. As these are dragged around by heat currents in the mantle below, they carry the continents with them, in a process of rearrangement that pushes some together while tearing others apart. The continents that we know today are fragments of the giant supercontinent Pangaea, which came together around 250 million years ago.

The supercontinent was surrounded by the immense Panthalassic Ocean, which evolved into the Pacific.

250 MYA

Make the landmasses move

LOST WORLDS

1 In the distant past the globe looked completely different, with strangely shaped landmasses in places that are now open sea. But over time the process of continental drift created a pattern of continents and oceans that has evolved into the world we know today.

385 MYA

The land at the heart of Pangaea was too far from the ocean to get much rain, so it was a vast sandy desert.

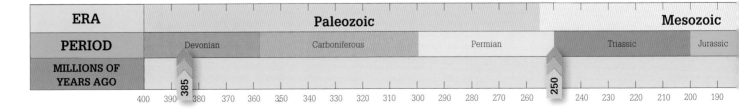

ERA	Paleozoic				Mesozoic	
PERIOD	Devonian	Carboniferous	Permian		Triassic	Jurassic
MILLIONS OF YEARS AGO	385			250		

400 390 380 370 360 350 340 330 320 310 300 290 280 270 260 250 240 230 220 210 200 190

ROCK REFINERY

Continental crust is made of lighter, paler rocks than those of the ocean floor. These originally formed as volcanoes erupted through oceanic crust, partly melting it to create a rock called andesite. Compared to oceanic basalt, this continental rock is not as rich in dark, heavy elements such as iron, so it is lighter.

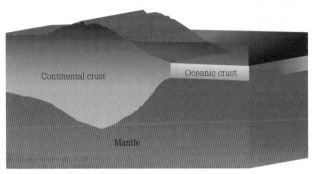

Continental crust

Oceanic crust

Mantle

FLOATING CONTINENTS

The continental rock erupted from andesitic volcanoes is around 20 percent lighter than the mantle rock beneath, so it floats on it. Over time, these rocky rafts have grown thicker and joined together to form continents. The highest parts of these landmasses have deep roots, and in some places the continental crust is 56 miles (90 km) thick, compared to a maximum of 7 miles (11 km) for oceanic crust.

The Atlantic Ocean started to open up in the early Cretaceous period, during the age of dinosaurs.

0 MYA

The continent of South America is still moving away from Africa, at the rate of 1.5 in (38 mm) per year.

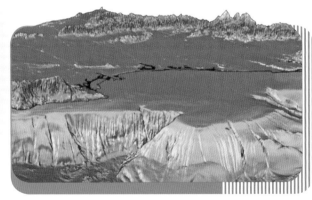

SHELF SEAS

The edge of a continent is not at its coast, but far offshore. This is because the fringes of the continents are cut away by the waves, creating continental shelves below shallow coastal seas less than 490 ft (150 m) deep. The shelf—shown here in green off the coast of California—is made of continental rock covered by thick layers of sand and mud. At its edge, the sea floor falls away down the continental slope to the ocean floor, which averages around 13,000 ft (4,000 m) deep.

Cenozoic

Cretaceous | Paleogene | Neogene

0

150 140 130 120 110 100 90 80 70 60 50 40 30 20 10

TIMELINE

Continental drift has been happening since continents were first formed more than 4 billion years ago, but even over the past 400 million years it has competely reshaped the world.

Rifts and trenches

Where tectonic plates are pulling apart, they create spreading rifts. These are mainly oceanic features that form new ocean floor at midocean ridges. Meanwhile other plates are pushing together, forcing one beneath another to form deep ocean-floor trenches. This destroys oceanic crust as fast as it is created, so the planet stays the same size.

MIDOCEAN RIDGES

Heat currents in the mantle rise and diverge near the planet's surface, dragging the brittle crust with them and ripping it apart to form long rifts. As a rift opens up, the pressure that keeps the mantle rock solid is reduced, allowing some to melt and erupt as liquid basalt lava. This solidifies in the rift, which then rips again, allowing more lava to erupt. On ocean floors, the lava builds up as mountain ranges, forming midocean ridges that may extend halfway around the globe.

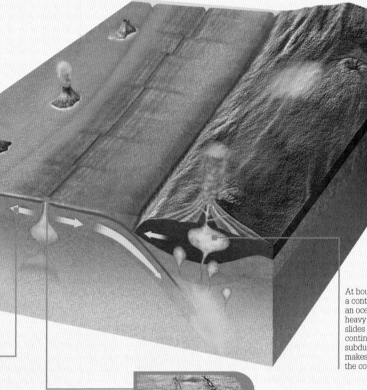

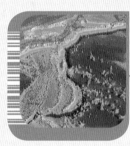

Where plates are pushing together, one dives beneath the other and melts back into the mantle. In oceans, this creates a deep trench in the ocean floor. This image based on satellite data shows the deepest, the Mariana Trench in the Pacific, as a curving dark blue line.

As new crust is added in the rift zone, the ocean floor expands. This is making the Atlantic wider each year, but in the Pacific the expansion is offset by ocean-floor destruction along trenches around the edge of the ocean.

At boundaries between a continental plate and an oceanic plate, the dense, heavy oceanic crust always slides beneath lighter continental crust. This subduction process makes volcanoes on the continent erupt.

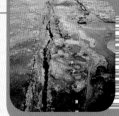

Iceland is a volcanic island that has formed on a highly active part of the Mid-Atlantic Ridge. The rift passes right through the island, which is getting slightly wider each year. The process opens up deep cracks in the rift zone, like the ones seen here.

BLACK SMOKERS

Seawater that seeps down through fissures in oceanic rift zones is superheated by contact with the hot rock. The high pressure allows it to reach temperatures of 750°F (400°C) or more; this enables it to dissolve various minerals in the rock before it erupts from the hydrothermal vents that pepper the rift. The sudden drop in pressure and temperature turns the minerals into clouds of solid particles that can look like black smoke.

CRUMPLED CONTINENTS

Where ocean floor plows beneath a continent, friction crumples the edge of the land into a series of mountain ridges. These mountains are often dotted with volcanoes that erupt over the plate boundary. The volcanoes are fueled by molten rock, created as oceanic sediments and water are carried down into the mantle by the descending plate; these change the chemistry of the hot rock so some of it melts and erupts as volcanic lava.

The Atlantic Ocean is 10 in (25 cm) wider than it was a century ago.

ISLAND ARCS

Plate boundaries where one slab of ocean floor is diving beneath another are marked by chains of volcanic islands called island arcs. These include the Lesser Antilles on the eastern edge of the Caribbean, seen here from space. They have been formed by volcanoes erupting from the plate boundary where the Atlantic Ocean floor is grinding beneath the Caribbean Plate.

SLIDING BOUNDARIES

In some places tectonic plates slide past each other, causing earthquakes but few volcanoes. There are thousands of these transform faults on the ocean floors, but the San Andreas Fault in California is the most famous on land. The western side is part of the Pacific Plate, sliding northwest relative to the North American Plate at about 1.4 in (3.5 cm) per year.

Earthquakes and tsunamis

In the 1960s, the United States set up a near-global network of sensors to detect earth-shaking nuclear bomb tests. But the sensors also monitored earthquakes. The data showed that nearly all earthquakes took place along midocean ridges and deep ocean trenches—what we now recognize as tectonic plate boundaries. It became clear that they were the result of movement along these fault lines.

CREEPING FRONTIERS

Earth's tectonic plates are always moving, every minute of every day, by a tiny amount. This means that the boundaries between the plates are always shifting slightly. Where this is happening at a steady rate, it causes the gradual creep that has offset the painted lines on this road. Movement like this causes frequent, minor earth tremors. But if the plates lock together the strain builds up until something snaps. This triggers an earthquake.

LOCK AND SNAP

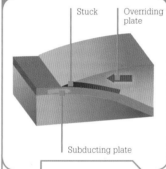

Stuck | Overriding plate

Subducting plate

Lock
Where one plate is moving against another, the rocks often lock together. Here, a plate of oceanic crust grinding beneath a continent is locked in the red zone.

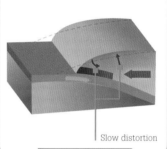

Slow distortion

Distort
Since the plates keep moving at the normal rate, this puts the locked section of the boundary under immense strain, distorting the rocks like a metal spring.

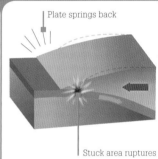

Plate springs back

Stuck area ruptures

Snap
Eventually the locked fault line snaps, and the distorted edge of the plate springs back to its original shape in a few seconds. The shock causes an earthquake.

EARTH SHOCK

Shock waves radiating from the earthquake focus shake the crust like ripples on a pond, so buildings crumble and collapse. Sometimes soft ground is liquefied by the tremors, so it behaves like wet sand and loses all its solidity. This happened in Niigata, Japan, in 1964, where tall buildings simply keeled over as the ground gave way beneath them.

EFFECTS	Barely detectable	Detected; not felt	Slight tremor	Distinct shaking
MAGNITUDE	0 1	2	3	4

TSUNAMI

If one tectonic plate plowing under another causes a lock-snap earthquake on the ocean floor, it generates a tsunami. As the overlying plate springs back up, it pushes the water into a heap that speeds across the ocean as a series of giant waves. These then surge ashore as immensely destructive walls of water. Here, the 2011 Japanese tsunami pours over the sea wall at the northern fishing port of Miyako.

テレトラック
MIYAKO

EARTHQUAKE ZONES

Some parts of the world are notorious for earthquakes, such as Indonesia, Japan, California, and southeast Europe. These earthquake zones lie on tectonic plate boundaries where the plates tend to lock together for many years before giving way. The worst earthquakes usually occur at boundaries where one plate is grinding beneath another, as in Japan, but California earthquakes are caused by one plate sliding sideways against the other.

MONITORING AND PREDICTION

Earthquakes are easy to measure using a seismograph such as this one to detect and record the seismic (earthquake) waves. But predicting an earthquake accurately is impossible. Some regions suffer them on a regular basis, and if history shows they occur roughly 80 years apart, then clearly an earthquake can be expected within 80 years of the last one. But the margin of error might be ten years either way, and scientists still have no way of narrowing this down.

RICHTER SCALE

Earthquakes are often measured using the Richter Scale of magnitude. Each increase in number indicates ten times as much shaking force, so an earthquake that measures 6 on the scale is ten times as powerful as a category 5 event—and a Richter Scale 7 earthquake is 100 times as powerful.

Moderate damage	Serious damage	Local destruction	Widespread chaos	Devastation

5   6   7   8   9

Building mountains

A mountain is not just a massive lump of high land. It is there for a reason. Most mountains are pushed up by the forces of plate tectonics. Colliding plates create crumple zones in continents, folding and thickening the crust to build ranges of fold mountains. Others form where the crust is stretched, so some parts slip down while others survive as highlands. Mountains can also be created by soft rock wearing away to expose isolated cores of much harder rock.

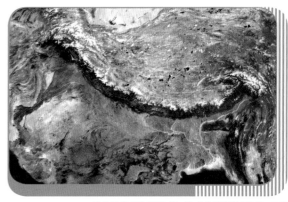

COLLIDING CONTINENTS

Where slabs of continental crust collide, the edges of both continents crumple to form broad mountain belts. The highest are the Himalayas and the high plateau of Tibet, seen here from space. They were created by India moving north to collide with Southeast Asia. India is still on the move, and the mountains are still rising.

WRINKLES

Where a slab of ocean floor is plowing beneath a continent, the edge of the continent is wrinkled into a series of folds to create a range of fold mountains. The most spectacular example of this process is the Andes, which are being pushed up by the Pacific Ocean floor grinding eastward beneath South America. At more than 4,300 miles (7,000 km) long they extend all along the western edge of the continent, forming the longest mountain range on land.

TOUGH SURVIVORS

During the seismic events that build mountains, molten rock often wells up from deep within the crust. It can erupt from volcanoes, or slowly solidify below ground to create a mass of hard, crystalline rock such as granite. Over time, the softer surrounding rock is worn away by erosion, slowly exposing the core. Devils Tower in Wyoming was probably formed in this way.

CRUMPLE ZONES

Many rocks are formed from layers of soft mud or sand that turn to stone. Mountain building causes massive crumpling and folding of these rock layers, or strata, often turning them on end or even upside down. The extreme pressure also squeezes the rock itself, compressing relatively soft strata into much harder, more durable rocks.

The Himalayas are rising at the rate of 0.2 in (5 mm) per year.

Only young by geological standards, the Andes are still being pushed upward and are some of the most rugged mountains on Earth.

RIFTS AND FAULTS

Continents can be stretched as well as squeezed. This fractures the rocks, creating faults that allow big blocks of crust to sink and form rift valleys. The regions between the valleys remain as block mountains, and often have steep cliffs marking the fault lines. The Basin and Range Province of the western United States was formed like this, with mountain ranges separated by long rift valleys.

ERODED STUMPS

Over time, all mountains are worn away by erosion. The softer their rocks—and the more severe the climate—the quicker they erode. Many ancient mountains have been reduced to rounded stumps, such as these in northwest Australia. If all mountain-building processes stopped, the continents would eventually be worn flat.

Volcanoes and geysers

Volcanic eruptions are the most dramatic of all geological events. Searingly hot molten rock flows downhill in rivers of fire, and vast ash clouds billow into the sky to blot out the Sun. Some volcanoes erupt quite often, so they are predictable. But others may lie dormant for centuries, then suddenly explode and produce avalanches of hot gas and rock that can wipe out entire cities.

RIFT VOLCANOES

Most volcanoes lie on the boundaries of Earth's tectonic plates. Where two plates are pulling apart, the pressure that keeps the hot rock below the crust solid is relaxed. Some of the rock melts, and erupts through the rift as liquid basalt lava. Most of these rift volcanoes erupt on the ocean floor along midocean ridges, but they also occur in Iceland, which lies on the Mid-Atlantic Ridge.

HOT SPOTS

Some volcanoes erupt over isolated hot spots beneath the crust. As the mobile plates slide over these hot spots, new volcanoes erupt while older ones fall extinct, forming island chains such as Hawaii. Kilauea volcano on Hawaii is the most active on Earth, while its neighbor Mauna Kea is higher than Everest when measured from its base on the ocean floor.

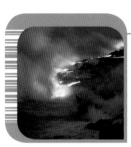

Fiery molten basalt erupted from Kilauea flows all the way to the coast, plunging into the ocean in clouds of steam.

The sticky lava does not flow far, so it builds up to form steep conical volcanoes.

Water and seafloor sediments are carried down into the mantle.

Some hot mantle rock melts and boils up through the crust.

LETHAL MIX

The most dangerous volcanoes erupt from plate boundaries where one plate is pushing beneath another, carrying seafloor sediments and water down into the mantle. The water lowers the melting point of the mantle rock, so it melts and erupts from volcanoes. The sediments make the lava more viscous so it does not flow easily, and also add a lot of gas—a deadly combination that causes violent, explosive eruptions.

STRATO-VOLCANOES

Many nonoceanic volcanoes are made up of layers of lava and ash. The sticky lava doesn't flow far, so it forms a steep cone. It may also solidify in the crater, sealing the volcano until increasing gas pressure makes it explode. Gas, molten rock, and fine volcanic ash are blasted into the air, but some of this scorching hot debris may surge down the flanks of the volcano. This debris forms the ash layers of the volcano.

CATACLYSM

Eruptions of island volcanoes can be hugely destructive. Such volcanoes form above broad magma chambers filled with molten rock. A massive eruption can empty the magma chamber, so its roof collapses. Seawater pours into the red-hot void and explodes with cataclysmic force, leaving a vast crater called a caldera. Around 3,600 years ago this happened to Santorini in the Aegean, seen here from space. The central caldera is 7.5 miles (12 km) long.

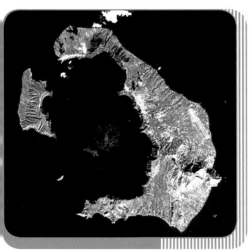

The lava that erupts from a stratovolcano has a temperature of about 1,560°F (850°C). If it cools rapidly enough it may form a solid plug in the crater.

As the lumpy, slow-flowing lava creeps down the steep slopes, it incinerates everything in its path. It often cools and solidifies before it reaches the bottom.

The cone of this type of volcano is built up from lava flows separated by layers of powdery ash and rock known as tephra. Every eruption adds another layer, so the volcano grows higher and higher.

HOT SPRINGS

If water touches hot rock below ground, it can bubble up as a hot spring. In some places, high pressure allows it to get much hotter than its usual boiling point, but eventually some is forced to the surface, so the pressure drops. The superheated water then boils and blasts out of the ground as a geyser.

VOLCANIC ASH

1 If an active volcano is plugged with solidified lava, pressure can build up until it explodes with the force of a nuclear bomb. This blows the top off the volcano, forming a plume of volcanic ash that rises high in the sky. But some often falls back and pours downhill as a high-speed pyroclastic flow.

Make the volcano explode

Most volcanoes form over magma chambers—underground pools of molten rock that has seeped up from beneath the crust. Magma accumulates in the chamber until rising pressure forces it to erupt.

Minerals & rocks

Massive erosion in
Monument Valley

Earth is a spinning ball of rock orbiting the Sun. The rock is made up of minerals, which are natural compounds of elements that were originally created by nuclear fusion in distant stars. Over time, the rocks on the land surface are shattered and dissolved by erosion, and their minerals are recycled to form other types of rocks. Eventually some rocks may even be dragged beneath the planet's crust, melted, and then recrystallized in the relentless process of the rock cycle.

Minerals

Minerals are the natural, usually solid substances that form rocks. Most are made up of elements that have reacted together to form chemical compounds. Often the results are quite unlike any of the ingredients, and they frequently take the form of beautiful crystals. Minerals can also contain elements in their pure form; these include the most valuable of all natural materials, such as precious metals.

CHEMICAL COMPOUNDS

Most minerals are chemical compounds, with the atoms of two or more elements joined together in a distinctive structure. One example is iron oxide, created when oxygen atoms link up with iron atoms. As with many minerals, this combines two very different elements, a metal and a gas, to make something quite unlike either—the granular, reddish substance we call rust.

Salt is made of sodium atoms and chlorine atoms linked together in the cubic structure of sodium chloride. This shape is echoed by the cubic form of the crystal.

CRYSTALS

Many minerals form crystals: geometric, gemlike structures with shapes that are defined by the way the atoms of the minerals fit together. Most crystals have complex shapes, but halite—better known as salt—forms crystals that are based on cubes. This mass of salt crystals encrusting rocks at the edge of a salt lake is really a mass of tiny cubic structures, created as salt water evaporated beneath the hot desert sun.

HYDROTHERMAL VEINS

When groundwater deep within the crust is heated to very high temperatures, it can dissolve a wide variety of minerals in the rocks. If the resulting solution is forced up through rock fissures and then cools, the minerals form sheets of crystals known as hydrothermal veins. Dissolved silica, for example, forms veins and nodules of quartz, which are often tinted by impurities to create beautifully colored crystals like this amethyst.

The blue in this painting by Michelangelo was made of ground-up azurite—the blue part of this lump of azurite and green malachite. Both are compounds of copper.

METALLIC MINERALS

Many minerals are made up of metal atoms linked to the atoms of other elements, although this is not at all obvious from their appearance. Common salt is one example; it is sodium chloride, formed from a metal (sodium) and a gas (chlorine). Others are corundum, made up of aluminum and oxygen, and galena (lead and sulfur). Many are very colorful, and for centuries they were the main ingredients of paints used by great artists.

NATIVE ELEMENTS

Some minerals consist of just one element. This can be accidental, as with this pure sulfur that has crystallized out of the gases erupting from a volcanic crater. But other elements resist forming chemical compounds with others, so they tend to stay pure. They include gold—so unwilling to react with anything at all that it is found as pure gold nuggets, and never loses its metallic luster.

METALS

A few metals such as gold and silver are found in pure, native form. The earliest metalworkers used these to make artifacts like this pure gold bracelet. But most metals occur only as minerals called ores. Over time people learned that these yielded pure metals if they were heated. They also found that mixing copper with tin created bronze—the tough, versatile metal that underpinned the first civilizations.

GEMSTONES

Some minerals are valuable gems. They include some of the hardest, such as this diamond. This is partly because they are almost indestructible, but also because their dense structure affects the way light passes through them. It makes them glitter and flash with a sparkle that cannot be matched by colored glass.

Rocks

All rocks are made of separate minerals that are mixed together like the ingredients of a cake. Some have been formed from molten mineral material—magma or lava—that has cooled and crystallized. Others are made from fragments of broken rock that have been cemented together. A few are built up from the remains of living things. Any of these rocks can be altered by intense heat or pressure so that they look quite different.

IGNEOUS ROCKS

When magma or lava cools and solidifies the minerals separate, and interlocking crystals are formed. This is visible in this magnified sample of a rock called gabbro viewed under polarized light that makes each mineral glow with a different color. The interlocking crystals make igneous rocks extremely hard.

BASALT AND GRANITE

The ingredients of igneous rocks depend on the nature of the original molten magma or lava. If it erupts from the mantle, deep below the crust, its minerals are rich in heavy metallic elements and cool to form heavy, dark rocks like basalt on the ocean floors. But if the magma erupts at the surface, it contains molten material from the crust that has fewer heavy metallic elements and forms lighter, paler continental rocks such as this granite.

SEDIMENTARY ROCKS

When existing rocks are broken down by weathering, the debris is carried away and laid down as sediments such as sand or mud. Over time these are compressed and cemented together by minerals to create sedimentary rocks such as this sandstone. They are quite soft, but harden with age.

The oldest rocks on Earth were formed more than 4 billion years ago.

ROCK STRATA

Beds of sedimentary rock are laid down horizontally to form layers called strata, with the oldest layer at the bottom. But these can be spectacularly buckled by earth movements, so they are tilted, tipped on end, or even turned upside down. The contorted layers are often visible in coastal cliffs, as seen here. The strata are often similar, but sometimes a sequence of very different sediments creates dramatic patterns.

Viewed under the intense magnification of an electron microscope, grains of chalk are revealed as clusters of tiny coccoliths—the stony skeletons of single-celled plankton that drifted in ancient oceans.

BIG BUILDUP

Some sedimentary rocks are formed by chemical reactions. Oolitic limestone is made up of tiny calcite "pearls" that formed long ago on the beds of warm, lime-saturated seas. Others are massive buildups of organic material. For example, the chalk on these sea cliffs was formed from the skeletons of billions of microscopic marine organisms during the age of the dinosaurs, whereas coal is made up of compressed plant material.

METAMORPHIC ROCKS

Intense pressure or heat can alter the nature of rocks, squeezing soft shale into hard slate, or cooking limestone to create marble. These metamorphic rocks often contain distinct crystalline layers formed by the pressure, as with this lump of highly compressed, folded gneiss. Such rocks include some of the oldest on the planet.

INTRUSIONS AND AUREOLES

Sometimes molten rock is squeezed up through cracks in sedimentary rocks, or between the strata, where it freezes as igneous intrusions as seen here. The hot molten rock may also cook the surrounding sedimentary rock to form "metamorphic aureoles" that are rich in valuable minerals.

Fossils

Some rocks contain traces of organisms that died long ago. Known as fossils, they are usually scattered bones, teeth, or shells that have been turned to stone. But some are beautifully preserved intact skeletons, and some even show traces of soft tissue. Fossils are our only evidence of extinct life, like the dinosaurs. They are also a very useful tool for dating rocks, and helping to unravel the whole history of the planet.

FOSSILIZATION

Most fossils are formed when the remains of a dead organism are buried in a soft, airless sediment such as mud. Without air they don't decay in the usual way, and are preserved. Over millions of years the sediment turns to rock, and dissolved minerals in the groundwater turn the organic material to stone. This fossil fern was formed like this, and was only revealed when the rock surrounding it was split open.

PERFECTLY PRESERVED

An animal's body usually falls apart soon after it dies, so only scattered hard parts such as the bones and teeth are fossilized. But sometimes an entire skeleton survives with all the bones in place. Even more rarely, some fossils preserve soft tissues such as skin and feathers—as seen in this fossil of the small feathered dinosaur *Microraptor*, found in China in 2003.

SUBFOSSILS

A fossil is technically any part of an organism that survives the normal processes of decay and is preserved. This includes things like ice-age mammoths found frozen in the Arctic, or this fly, which became trapped in sticky tree sap that later hardened into amber. Sometimes described as subfossils, these may preserve every detail of the animal's body.

TRACE FOSSILS

Some fossils are no more than casts of decayed organic material, although these trace fossils can be very detailed. Others preserve footprints such as these, which were left in wet volcanic ash in Tanzania, Africa, roughly 3.5 million years ago. They may not look like much, but they are actually very exciting because they tell us that some of our earliest ancestors walked upright. Their footprints also show how they walked, and how tall they were.

THE FOSSIL RECORD

As long ago as 330 bce, the Greek philosopher Aristotle realized that fossils were the remains of ancient life. But their significance was not understood until the 19th century, when scientists recognized that they were evidence of the development of life through the ages. At first this "fossil record" was very incomplete, but every day more fossils such as this dinosaur bone are discovered, disproving old theories and giving us a deeper insight into how life on Earth has evolved.

DATING TOOLS

The most spectacular fossils are things like dinosaur skeletons, but these are rare. The most common fossils are seashells like these ammonites, which are very useful because geologists can use them to date rocks. There were many species of ammonite that survived for relatively short periods of time, but they were very widespread. So if the same species is found in different rocks in different places, the rocks are probably the same age.

The rock cycle

When rocks are raised above sea level they start to be worn down by erosion, creating fragments that are carried away and deposited as sediments. Over vast spans of time the sediments are hardened into sedimentary rock, which is often eroded in turn. But it may also be compressed and heated to form metamorphic rock, and even melted and turned into igneous rock that undergoes the whole process all over again.

SHATTERED AND DISSOLVED

In cold climates rocks are shattered by the freeze-thaw process. Rock fissures fill with rainwater that then freezes; this gradually wedges the cracks apart until lumps of rock fall away, creating scree slopes like these in northern England. Meanwhile glacial ice and sand-loaded flowing water gouge deep valleys, while rainwater attacks minerals in the rocks so they dissolve or crumble to form clay and sand.

STRIPPED BARE

In desert zones the wind picks up dry sand and hurls it at exposed rock like an industrial sandblaster, carving it into dramatic shapes. Rare torrential rainstorms cause flash floods loaded with rocks and sand that rip through gullies, scouring deep canyons like this one in Arizona. Eventually just a few areas are left above the plain as isolated mesas and buttes.

RECYCLING THE ROCKS

Rocky debris eroded from the uplands is carried downhill by rivers and deposited on floodplains, lake beds, and ultimately in the sea. Wind-blown sand is piled up in dunes, while coastal sediments form beaches and soft sea beds. Over time, these soft sediments may be compressed into sedimentary rocks. Some may then be buried, metamorphosed, and eventually melted, to re-erupt in the form of volcanic lava.

Even the hardest rocks are slowly ground to dust by the relentless rock cycle.

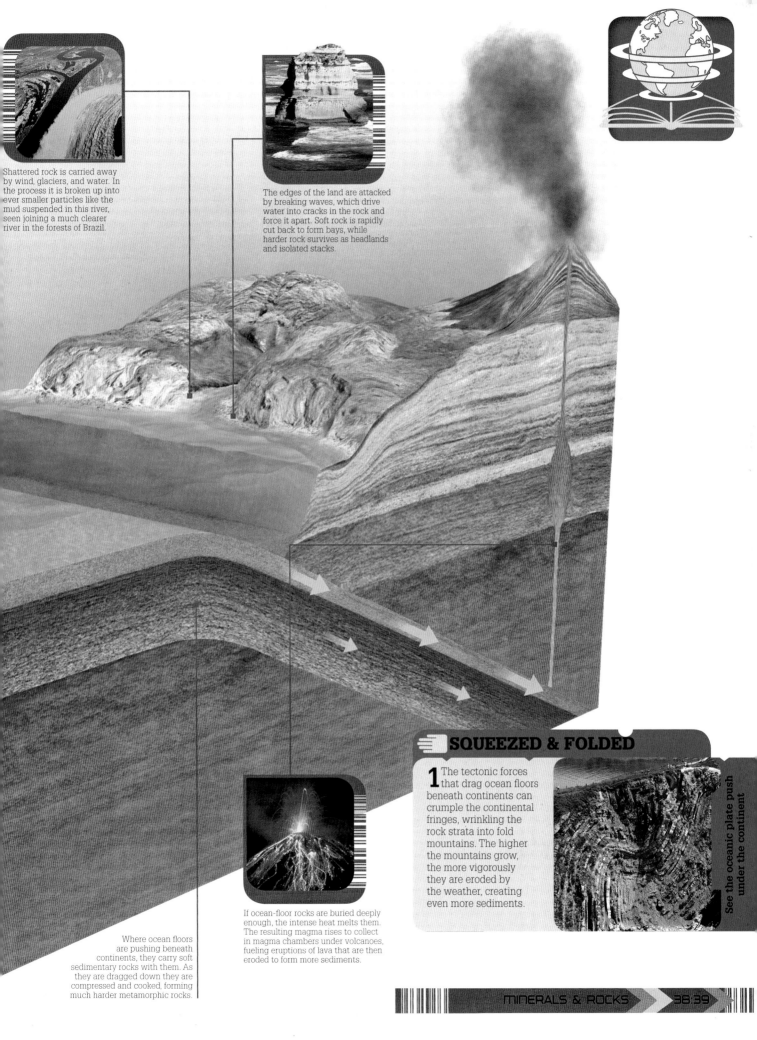

Shattered rock is carried away by wind, glaciers, and water. In the process it is broken up into ever smaller particles like the mud suspended in this river, seen joining a much clearer river in the forests of Brazil.

The edges of the land are attacked by breaking waves, which drive water into cracks in the rock and force it apart. Soft rock is rapidly cut back to form bays, while harder rock survives as headlands and isolated stacks.

Where ocean floors are pushing beneath continents, they carry soft sedimentary rocks with them. As they are dragged down they are compressed and cooked, forming much harder metamorphic rocks.

If ocean-floor rocks are buried deeply enough, the intense heat melts them. The resulting magma rises to collect in magma chambers under volcanoes, fueling eruptions of lava that are then eroded to form more sediments.

SQUEEZED & FOLDED

1 The tectonic forces that drag ocean floors beneath continents can crumple the continental fringes, wrinkling the rock strata into fold mountains. The higher the mountains grow, the more vigorously they are eroded by the weather, creating even more sediments.

See the oceanic plate push under the continent

Caves

The most spectacular caves form in limestone terrain as the rock is dissolved by rainwater. As the water seeps down through the rock it turns narrow cracks into crevices and fissures. These may then grow into stream-swallowing, vertical shafts that are linked to complex networks of underground caves and broad caverns, often adorned with fantastic natural features created by the dripping, mineral-loaded water.

ACID ATTACK

All rainwater is slightly acidic, so it dissolves lime. It eats away limestone that is exposed at the surface, enlarging its natural joints to form a "limestone pavement" of blocks (clints) divided by deep fissures (grykes). Water drains through these fissures and slowly dissolves the rock below to create limestone caves.

SWALLOW HOLES

Surface streams are rare in limestone regions, because all the rainwater seeps down through the cracks in the soluble rock. However, in places, water draining off other types of rock forms a stream, and if this flows onto the limestone it may disappear down an enlarged fissure called a swallow hole or sinkhole. The water sometimes cascades into the void as a spectacular waterfall, and continues as an underground stream flowing through a network of caves.

UNDERGROUND RIVERS

The water that drains into fissured limestone dissolves vertical shafts and long horizontal caves, flowing as underground streams for long distances before emerging in valleys as springs or "resurgences." Some of the caves become flooded to the ceiling, especially after heavy rain. In some places several streams may join together to feed a big, underground river that flows through broad passages, like this in the Hang Son Doong cave in Vietnam. Eventually, the river emerges from the base of a limestone cliff.

VAST CAVERNS

Cave ceilings often collapse, enlarging narrow, low passages into bigger chambers that may contain underground lakes. Some of these develop into vast, yawning caverns, as big as cathedrals and just as spectacular. Here, two cave explorers in the limestone region of Gunung Mulu National Park in Sarawak, Malaysia, are dwarfed by the sheer scale of Deer Cave—an immense cavern that is up to 554 ft (169 m) wide and 410 ft (125 m) high.

STONE SCULPTURES

The water that seeps through limestone often contains as much lime as it can dissolve. When it drips into a cave, the air in the cave slightly changes the chemistry of the water so that some of the dissolved lime crystallizes to form solid calcite. This clings to where the water is dripping or flowing over the rock. Over centuries, it builds up to form hanging stalactites, stalagmites growing up from the cave floor, and other amazing natural stone sculptures.

CRYSTAL CAVES

Some caves contain glittering crystals, formed by minerals in the groundwater. These giant gypsum crystals in the Naica Mine, Mexico, were created over millions of years from minerals that were once dissolved in the volcanic hot water that filled the cave. Discovered in 2000, they are the largest known crystals in the world.

MEXICAN CENOTES

The Yucatán peninsula in Mexico is an ancient, uplifted coral reef—and, like all coral reefs, it is made of limestone. As with other limestone landscapes, the surface water drains into the rock, creating networks of caves and caverns. Some of the caverns have collapsed to form cavities that are open to the sky, and contain beautiful sunken lakes. These cenotes were the only sources of drinking water in the past, and to the ancient Mayan civilization they were sacred places.

Weather & climate

The lowest layer of Earth's atmosphere is constantly on the move, driving the dynamic and sometimes dramatic phenomena we call weather. The air currents carry warm air toward the polar regions and cold polar air toward the tropics, keeping the planet inhabitable over most of its surface. But there are still big differences between the world's climates, which range from the hot, steamy luxuriance of tropical rain forests to the arid sterility of icebound polar deserts.

Weather like this tornado can be violently destructive

Climate zones

Earth's climate zones are defined by how the Sun's rays strike different parts of the planet. This affects the temperature of the atmosphere, generating air currents that carry heat. These air currents create wet regions and deserts, and drive the prevailing winds that carry weather systems around the globe. Most climates also change with the seasons, and some undergo a complete transformation.

Sun's rays strike the surface obliquely in the polar regions, so they are dispersed and weakened

Sun's rays strike the surface directly in the tropics, so they are more concentrated

SOLAR ENERGY
The way that the Sun's rays strike the globe means that solar energy is spread over a much wider area in the polar regions than it is near the equator. This gives it a less intense heating effect, even in summer, and is the basic reason why the far north and far south are so much colder than the tropics.

SEASONAL SHIFTS
As Earth orbits the Sun once a year, the temperate and polar regions move closer to the Sun for several months, then move farther away. This causes the seasons. They are most extreme in the Arctic and Antarctic, where there is virtually permanent darkness in winter and permanent daylight in summer, but there are also dramatic wet and dry seasons in the tropics.

DELVING DEEPER

Earth spins on an axis that is tilted at 23.5 degrees from the vertical. As it orbits the Sun it always leans the same way, so in June the North Pole is tilted toward the Sun, while the South Pole is tilted away. As a result, the Northern Hemisphere is heated more intensely than the Southern Hemisphere, so it is summer in the north and winter in the south. Six months later the situation is reversed.

December: summer in south

Autumn in south; spring in north

Autumn in north; spring in south

June: summer in north

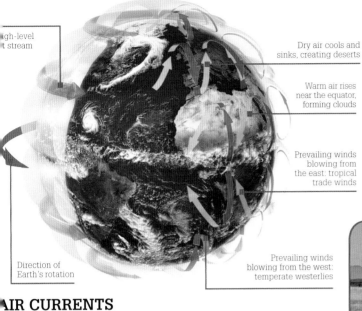

gh-level
t stream

Dry air cools and
sinks, creating deserts

Warm air rises
near the equator,
forming clouds

Prevailing winds
blowing from
the east: tropical
trade winds

Prevailing winds
blowing from the west:
temperate westerlies

Direction of
Earth's rotation

AIR CURRENTS

Tropical sunshine warms moist air in the lowest layer of the atmosphere. The air rises, forming clouds and rain to create a rain-forest climate. It flows away from the equator, cools, and sinks; this stops clouds from forming, and creates a desert climate. Other air currents exist farther north and south. They also drive the prevailing winds that blow from a certain direction most of the time. At high altitudes the difference in temperature between air masses creates strong winds called jet streams.

PREVAILING WINDS

As air currents circulate through the atmosphere, Earth's spin makes them swerve off course, driving the prevailing winds. In the tropics, air moving toward the equator at sea level swerves west, becoming the light trade winds that blow from the east. Further north and south, air moving toward the polar regions swerves east to become stronger prevailing winds that blow from the west.

OCEANS AND CONTINENTS

Oceans heat up and cool down more slowly than continents. This gives nearby land areas a mild oceanic climate, with cool summers and relatively warm winters. Continental regions like central Asia have far hotter summers and colder winters—and because they are so far from the oceans, they also get far less rain.

MONSOONS

As continents heat up in summer they heat the air above, so it rises and draws in moist air from the oceans. In winter they chill down, cooling the air so it sinks and pushes dry air out toward the oceans. In Asia this reversal creates the monsoons that bring heavy rain and floods to India in summer, and dry weather in winter.

MOUNTAIN CLIMATES

Temperature drops with altitude, so the climate on a mountain peak is colder than the climate at sea level in the same region. This is why Mount Kilimanjaro in east Africa is capped with snow, even though it lies close to the equator. Anyone who climbs it from the warm lowlands passes through a series of climate zones that resemble the ones you might pass through on a journey from the tropics to the Arctic.

Wind and rain

The weather is driven by the heat of the Sun. Heat makes air expand and rise, creating patches of low atmospheric pressure. Surrounding air flows into these low-pressure zones as local winds. Heat also turns water to water vapor, which is carried up by the rising air. As it rises it forms clouds, which lead to rain. Prevailing winds carry these weather systems around the globe, transferring water from the oceans to the continents.

CLOUDS

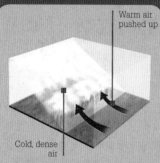

As the sea and land absorb solar energy, they radiate heat that warms the lower atmosphere. Meanwhile, water evaporates from the surface into the warm air. The warm, moist air expands and rises, cooling until the invisible water vapor condenses into the water droplets that form clouds. These can form at various altitudes, from low-level clouds like this cumulus to high, wispy cirrus made of tiny ice crystals.

TYPES OF CLOUD FORMATION

Warm air pushed up

Cold, dense air

Cloud forming

Rising warm air

Rising air cools

Sinking air warms up

Frontal clouds
Broad belts of cloud are created when a mass of warm moist air meets cold dense air at a weather "front." The warm air is pushed up and cools to create clouds.

Convective clouds
When moist air is heated by the warm ground below, air rises by convection to form clouds. These range from fluffy-looking cumulus to giant storm clouds.

Orographic clouds
If air has to pass over a mountain, it must rise. This is called orographic lifting. As the air is forced upward it expands and cools to form clouds over the peaks.

RAIN

Clouds are made of tiny airborne water droplets—or ice crystals at higher altitudes. These collide and join up to form bigger droplets, which collide in turn and grow even bigger. If they reach a size of about $\frac{1}{50}$ in (0.5 mm), they are heavy enough to fall as rain. This is often triggered by moist air being pushed upward, so it cools and condenses into more water droplets.

SWIRLING CYCLONES

Where warm, moist air is rising it creates areas of low atmospheric pressure called depressions or cyclones. Air flows in to replace the rising air, spiraling like water flowing into a drain. Rising, cooling water vapor forms clouds in spiral patterns that trace the airflow. They swirl clockwise in the Southern Hemisphere, as in this satellite image, and counterclockwise in the Northern Hemisphere. These clouds often bring persistent rain.

ANTICYCLONES

Low-pressure cyclones created by warm, rising air are separated by areas of cooler, denser air. Since the air is denser it exerts more atmospheric pressure. These high-pressure systems are called anticyclones. The dense air sinks, swirling in the opposite direction from cyclones. The sinking air stops moist air from rising and forming clouds, so an anticyclone usually brings clear skies. Long spells of fine weather in temperate regions are usually caused by slow-moving anticyclones.

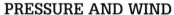

PRESSURE AND WIND

Air is pushed out of high-pressure zones and drawn into low-pressure zones. It spirals out of one and into the other, creating local winds that keep changing as the weather systems pass overhead. The bigger the pressure difference between the high-pressure zone and its neighboring low-pressure zone, the faster and stronger the wind. This is why a "deep low" on the weather map—a zone of very low atmospheric pressure—usually means that a storm is on the way.

THE FRONT LINE

Weather systems such as cyclones are carried by the prevailing winds. In the polar regions and tropics they are carried west, and in temperate regions they are carried east. Since cyclones bear rain, those places that lie on the oceanic front line facing the prevailing wind, such as western Ireland, have very wet climates. As the weather systems are swept inland their moisture is gradually used up, so regions farther from the oceanic front line have drier climates.

MICROCLIMATES

Local geography can have a big influence on the weather. High ridges facing the prevailing wind tend to catch the rain, so they are very wet on the windward side and dry on the leeward side. This effect is evident on this satellite image of Hawaii—the rain-bearing wind blowing from the east makes the right-hand side of each high-peaked island lush and green while the other is dry and brown. Other microclimate effects include very cold "frost pockets," created when sinking cold air flows off high land and settles in valleys.

Extreme weather

The weather is powered by solar energy—and the more energy, the more extreme the weather. The Sun's heat builds huge clouds that deluge the landscape with rain. It can generate thunderstorms, hail, howling hurricanes, and screaming tornadoes. These storms and the resulting floods are among the most destructive of all natural events.

Intense heat builds giant storm clouds that keep growing upward, spreading at the top when they reach the stratosphere. They store vast amounts of moisture and energy.

Powerful updrafts inside storm clouds toss ice crystals up and down so they gather layers of ice and become hailstones. This giant hailstone has been sliced in half to reveal the layers.

Static electricity generated by swirling air charges up storm clouds like giant, million-volt batteries. The charge flashes to earth as lightning, releasing the shockwave we call thunder.

A storm cloud can release vast amounts of water in a cloudburst. If this falls on a small area it may sweep downhill in a flash flood that destroys everything in its path.

TORNADOES

Updrafts swirling into an extra-massive rotating storm cloud can generate the spiral vortex of a tornado. The wind sucked into the rising air column can reach speeds of 310 mph (500 km/hr) or more. Combined with the updraft effect, it can be powerful enough to toss a car in the air or rip the roof off a house. It affects only a small area at a time, but keeps moving, cutting a swathe of devastation across the landscape.

On March 18, 1925, a single tornado that tore through three states killed 695 people.

SUPERCELL

1 A tornado begins life as a big storm cloud, built up by powerful currents of rising air. If the wind at high altitudes is blowing in a different direction from the surface wind, it can make the air currents start spiraling upward, creating a huge, swirling cloud mass called a supercell.

See a supercell

VORTEX

2 As the rising air starts to spin it forms a funnel of dark cloud that gradually extends down to the ground, creating a tornado. Low-level air rushing into the rising vortex swirls up into the supercell, carrying dust and debris with it and spitting it out the sides of the deadly spiral.

Control the path of a tornado

HURRICANES

The high surface temperatures of tropical oceans cause hurricanes—immensely powerful storms that revolve around centers of very low pressure created by rising warm, moist air. They generate winds of up to 186 mph (300 km/hr), but the eye of a hurricane, shown here, is eerily calm.

Rivers, lakes, and wetlands

Rainwater and melting snow draining off the landscape flow in streams and rivers that carve away the uplands to form valleys. The water carries the products of weathering away as sand and mud, which is deposited as sediments in the lowlands. This shifts rocky material from the uplands to the lowlands and the sea. It is a crucial part of the rock cycle, but it also shapes the landscape and the nature of streams and rivers that flow through it, as well as the lakes and wetlands that they feed.

VALLEY NETWORK
As streams and rivers flow downhill the erode V-shaped valleys in the hillside. These join up to create dendritic pattern that resemble the twigs and branches of a tree—like the valley networks in th snowy mountain landscape, seen from space. All the rock that is eroded from th valleys is swept away into the lowland.

FLOODPLAINS
The land around the middle reaches of a river is often very fertile, with broad floodplains created from sediment deposited in the valley during seasonal floods. The floodwater spreads out to form a broad, shallow lake, allowing fine sediment to settle on the land on either side of the river channel. This sediment is usually rich in plant nutrients, so the soil that it forms is very fertile. It makes excellent farmland—provided the floods can be controlled.

UPLAND STREAMS
Streams and rivers that drain off hills and mountains have fast-flowing upper courses with cascading waterfalls and rocky rapids. The rapidly flowing water can shift heavy stones, so the stream beds are often gravelly. Some even contain big boulders rolled downhill by seasonal floods.

LAKES AND WETLANDS

Most lakes form in natural depressions. They are usually fed by one or more streams, and most also have an outlet stream. When the water is warm and rich in nutrients, it is gradually overgrown with reeds and other wetland plants to form marshes and swamps. But cool, nutrient-poor upland lakes like this one are almost weed-free, and have beautifully clear water.

MEANDERS

When a river flows around a series of bends, it tends to cut away the bank on the outside of each bend while depositing sediment on the inside. This gradually makes its course more sinuous, so it flows across its floodplain in broad loops called meanders. Eventually a loop can become so extreme that the river breaks through, leaving the loop isolated as an oxbow lake—seen here on the left of this aerial view of the Amazon.

The Mississippi Delta has distorted the Earth's crust with its weight.

ESTUARIES

Most rivers flow to the sea. Here the salt in seawater makes mud particles in the river clump together and settle to form the broad mudflats of an estuary, especially on shores with a big tidal rise and fall. As the tide rises, the river flow often backs up, but as it falls the water drains rapidly out of the estuary, cutting deep channels through the gleaming mud.

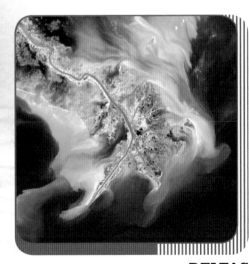

DELTAS

Many rivers carry sediment out to sea and dump it in very thick layers to form a delta. The water flows over this in streams called distributaries, which have different patterns depending on factors such as the tides. Well-defined, long distributaries are characteristic of "bird's foot" deltas, such as the Mississippi Delta seen in this satellite image.

Snow, glaciers, and ice sheets

If the air is cold enough, the moisture in clouds falls as snow rather than rain. This may melt to form rivers, but if it stays frozen it slowly turns to ice and flows downhill as glaciers. In polar regions the ice forms thick ice sheets that can completely bury the land, and even the oceans freeze over.

High-level clouds are made of microscopic ice crystals, which can join up to form six-sided snowflakes. These may then clump together to form the fluffy masses of crystals that fall as snow.

In cold climates some snow never melts. It builds up over the years, and its great weight compresses the lower layers, welding the snow crystals into solid ice. This creates glaciers, ice caps, and ice sheets.

CREEPING GLACIERS

Most glaciers begin life high in the mountains. Snow builds up in a rocky basin—a cirque or corrie—and turns to ice. The ice overflows the rim of the basin and creeps downhill, continually reshaping itself to flow over humps and around bends. Most glaciers cover just a few yards (meters) a day, but have massive erosive power, cutting deep U-shaped valleys and carrying vast amounts of rock debris away to lower altitudes.

GLACIAL EROSION

See what's happening inside a moving glacier

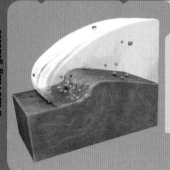

1 A glacier erodes deep valleys and hollows, and carves the landscape into smooth rounded shapes with scratches and grooves. It does this partly by abrasion—thanks to rocks stuck in the moving ice—and partly by freezing to the rock and ripping its surface away on the downflow side.

The ice at the base of the East Antarctic ice sheet is more than 400,000 years old.

TUMBLED ROCK

2 A mountain glacier creeps downhill until the point where the ice front melts as fast as it moves forward. It then stays in the same place, building up a "moraine" of rock carried by the ice. If the glacier melts away, it leaves a U-shaped valley with heaped moraines and thick layers of sediment.

Make the glacier melt and move downhill

ICEBERGS

In the polar regions many glaciers flow all the way to the coast. The snout of the glacier floats on the sea, where the tidal rise and fall makes big slabs of ice break off and float away as icebergs. This means that icebergs are made of freshwater ice, not sea ice. Most are 50–660 ft (15–200 m) long, but some tabular icebergs that break off Antarctic ice shelves are colossal—one found in 1956 was bigger than Belgium!

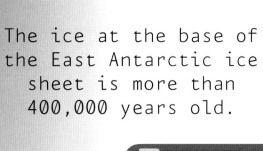

ICE SHEETS

Greenland and Antarctica are covered by immensely thick ice sheets built up from compacted snow over many thousands of years. The Antarctic ice sheet is up to 2.8 miles (4.5 km) deep, and in places it extends over the sea as thick ice shelves with icy cliffs up to 164 ft (50 m) high.

PACK ICE

On polar oceans the sea surface freezes, eventually forming a fractured mass of pack ice. There is always pack ice around the North Pole, although there is less than there used to be. In the Southern Ocean the sea area that freezes over in winter effectively doubles the size of Antarctica.

Changing climates

Earth's climates have been changing ever since the planet formed. The continents are always on the move, so their positions on the globe change; this also affects warm and cold ocean currents. The way Earth orbits the Sun varies according to predictable cycles, causing ice ages. Most recently, human activities have increased the greenhouse effect that keeps the planet warm, and this could trigger the most dramatic climate change of all.

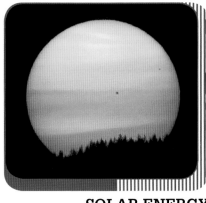

SOLAR ENERGY

Some 3.6 billion years ago there was far more carbon dioxide in the atmosphere than there is now. It created a powerful greenhouse effect—the insulation that keeps the planet warm. But the Sun was radiating 25 percent less energy than it produces today, so the temperature was much the same as it is now. Over time, the extra carbon dioxide was turned into carbonate rocks such as limestone—and this reduced the greenhouse effect at about the same rate as the Sun warmed up.

ORBITAL CYCLES

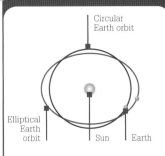

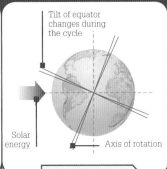

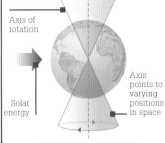

Shape
Variations in the shape of Earth's orbit cause regular climate cycles. It changes from elliptical to circular over a 100,000-year cycle, which affects its distance from the Sun.

Tilt
Over 42,000 years the tilt of Earth's axis varies from 21.6 ° to 24.5 °. The more tilt, the more extreme the seasons, with hotter summers and colder winters.

Wobble
A 25,800-year cycle makes Earth's axis point to different parts of space. Together with the other cycles, this is linked to the advance and retreat of ice ages.

COOLING DOWN

We are living in a warm period of an ice age. During the last cold period, which ended about 12,000 years ago, glaciers extended across much of northern Eurasia and North America. When they retreated they left dramatic landscapes like this glaciated valley in northern England. The Southern Hemisphere was less affected because most of it is ocean. But there are even traces of ancient ice in the Sahara—a legacy of when Africa lay at the South Pole.

THE BIG FREEZE

According to some scientists, the planet endured a near-catastrophic ice age roughly 650 million years ago. This period is known as the "Snowball Earth" because the entire globe was frozen over, including all the oceans, and the land at the equator was as cold as modern-day Antarctica. The big freeze lasted for 10 million years. It was followed by an equally dramatic thaw—possibly due to an enhanced greenhouse effect caused by a buildup of carbon dioxide erupted by volcanoes. But the whole theory is still fiercely debated.

CATASTROPHES

Very occasionally, colossal volcanoes throw so much dust and gas into the atmosphere that they change the climate. This probably happened in India 65 million years ago, when a series of gigantic eruptions spilled molten rock over a vast area. This could have wiped out the dinosaurs, but others blame an asteroid impact in what is now Mexico. Either or both events could have caused catastrophic climate change and a mass extinction.

WARMING UP

We are now in a period of rapid global warming, which climate scientists agree is being caused by the large quantities of carbon dioxide that are released into the atmosphere. This increases the greenhouse effect that keeps the planet warm, so it's getting warmer. Most of the carbon dioxide is created by burning fossil fuels based on coal, oil, and natural gas, but much is also being released by felling and burning forests.

SHRINKING GLACIERS

The effects of climate change are already becoming evident. The Arctic sea ice is only half as thick as it was 50 years ago, and its area is shrinking by 8 percent each year. This is bad news for polar bears. Frozen ground in the Arctic is melting, releasing methane gas that speeds up the warming process. Some fear that polar ice sheets are becoming unstable; if so, they could dump enough ice in the oceans to make sea levels rise dramatically, drowning coastal cities.

Elephants cross a
swamp in Botswana

Earth is unique because it supports life. But life is not just an addition to the planet—it influences its geology and structure. Some types of rock would not exist without it, and living things also contribute to the erosion process that is fundamental to the rock cycle. Many landscapes such as forests and grasslands are defined by the life that has colonized them. So life—or the biosphere—is as much a part of planet Earth as its rocks, oceans, and atmosphere.

Origins of life

When Earth formed about 4.6 billion years ago it was an inferno of hot and molten rock. But among the elements in its rocks were all the ingredients of life—especially carbon, which can form complex organic molecules such as proteins. Once the crust was cool enough for oceans to form, the stage was set for the chemical reactions that created the first self-replicating organisms.

IN THE BEGINNING

The earliest organisms on Earth probably resembled the microscopic, single-celled archaea that still live on the fringes of hot springs such as this one in Yellowstone National Park. They use chemical energy to turn simple chemicals into sugar, which they use to fuel their lives. Such life forms developed in warm, shallow water around 3.8 billion years ago, following a series of chemical reactions that formed the ingredients of proteins.

SOLAR POWER

Around 3.5 billion years ago the archaea gave rise to a form of bacteria that used solar energy to make sugar from water and carbon dioxide. Today this process—photosynthesis—is the main source of all the food produced on Earth. Similar cyanobacteria still live in the oceans, and as colonies called stromatolites in shallow coastal lagoons like these in western Australia.

VITAL OXYGEN

At first, Earth's atmosphere did not contain any free oxygen. It was all produced over about 2 billion years by cyanobacteria—resembling these modern *Spirulina*—as a by-product of photosynthesis. Since animals need oxygen, cyanobacteria made animal life possible. Oxygen also produces the ozone that protects land animals from deadly ultraviolet radiation.

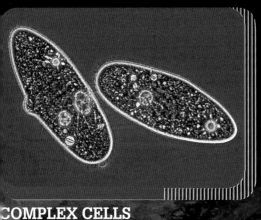

COMPLEX CELLS

Archaea and bacteria are simple cell membranes containing fluids. But roughly 2.2 billion years ago they developed into more complex cells, each with a nucleus and special structures for tasks such as turning sugar into energy. At first they were all single cells like this modern *Paramecium*, but by 1.2 billion years ago they were forming colonies.

MULTICELLULAR LIFE

Over time, identical cells living together in colonies started to take on specialized functions. This marked the beginning of multicellular life with special cells for different jobs, such as nerve cells and muscle cells. In turn this permitted the development of big organisms with a clear shape, like this marine flatworm. Around 540 million years ago this led to the appearance of most of the major groups of living things.

PRODUCERS AND CONSUMERS

Some organisms such as plants can produce food from carbon dioxide and water, and use it to build their tissues. Others such as animals and fungi cannot do this, but must consume ready-made food and digest it, recycling the products to build their own tissues. These producers and consumers form a web of life in which they all depend on each other—an ecosystem. There are many types of ecosystems, but they are all part of the global ecosystem, or biosphere.

BIODIVERSITY

Competition for scarce resources favors the survival of the fittest, so any lucky individual that has some advantage will be more likely to survive and breed. This process, known as natural selection, drives the evolution of new life forms. It has resulted in a spectacular diversity of life, with many millions of species.

Aquatic life

Water is the perfect environment for life. It is vital to the body chemistry of living things, so it is not surprising that life probably began in shallow seas. Most of the life on Earth still lives in the water of oceans, lakes, and rivers, where it has evolved into a spectacular variety of forms, ranging from microscopic plankton to giant fish.

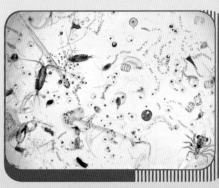

PLANKTON SWARMS

Nearly all ocean life relies on the food produced by microscopic phytoplankton that drift in the sunlit surface waters. Here they use photosynthesis to make sugar from dissolved carbon dioxide and water. They are eaten by swarms of tiny creatures called zooplankton, which include the young of animals such as crabs and clams. Many live in deeper water during the day, but swim to the surface at night to feed.

FOOD CHAIN

Drifting plankton are eaten by small fish such as herring. These are preyed upon by bigger fish including tuna, which are hunted in turn by sharks and other top predators. There are also huge plankton-eaters such as manta rays and whales. Meanwhile, scavengers on the sea floor polish off the remains of the dead.

THE DEEP

Below about 656 ft (200 m) there is not enough light for photosynthesis, so there are no living phytoplankton. This means there is little to eat, so the twilight and dark zones of the deep ocean support relatively few animals. Most deepwater fish, like this viperfish, survive by eating each other, seizing their prey with fearsomely long teeth.

CHEMICAL ENERGY

Mineral-rich hot springs on the ocean floors support animal communities that rely on chemical-processing microbes to make food. They include these giant tube worms, which may grow to 8 ft (2.4 m) long. The worms absorb the enriched water and supply it to food-making colonies of bacteria living in their bodies.

Despite covering only a small area, coral reefs support a quarter of all known marine species.

CORAL REEFS

The clear waters of tropical oceans contain little phytoplankton. However, very similar organisms live in the tissues of reef-building corals, where they make food by photosynthesis. The corals use this to fuel their growth, and the resulting coral reefs provide homes for a wonderful diversity of marine life. They are dazzlingly beautiful, but seriously threatened by climate change.

LAKES AND PONDS

Freshwater lake and pond life is similar to sea life, but plants play an important part, especially in the warm, fertile lowland waters favored by fish such as this pike. By contrast, cool, nutrient-poor upland lakes support relatively little life of any kind—although they are ideal for animals that need a lot of oxygen because cool water always contains more oxygen than warm water.

STREAMS AND RIVERS

Running water creates a very different habitat from a lake. The flow normally makes life impossible for plankton, and seasonal variations in the flow make it difficult for many other organisms, too. But a fast flow adds oxygen, allowing aquatic insects and fish such as trout to thrive. Streams flowing over hard rock have few dissolved minerals and few plant nutrients, while those that flow over softer rock are richer.

Forests

On land, areas with enough rainfall or permanently moist ground are taken over by trees, forming forests. These have different features depending on the climate and plants involved, but they all share one thing in common: dense tree growth. This is often so thick that the treetops almost touch, creating a continuous canopy. The trees shelter communities of smaller plants, fungi, and animals of all kinds. The wide variety of species interact to form some of the world's richest ecosystems.

TREE TAKEOVER

A forest is the result of a process called ecological succession, which starts when a piece of completely bare ground sprouts a few weeds. These pioneer plants are replaced by bigger, lusher plants that slowly give way to bushes and short-lived species of trees. Finally, longer-lived trees move in as the "climax vegetation"—so-called because nothing replaces them except younger trees of the same type. Every time a clearing is created by old trees falling, or by a wildfire as seen here, the process starts again.

THE NORTHERN TAIGA

Vast swaths of the far north are covered by dense boreal forests, or taiga. Most of the trees are very hardy needle-leaved evergreens such as pine and spruce. Their frostproof leaves shed snow easily, and since they are evergreen, they are ready for photosynthesis whenever there is enough sunshine. These forests are home to animals such as moose and wolves, which are tough enough to survive the harsh winters.

DECIDUOUS FORESTS

To the south of the taiga lie the deciduous forests. Their trees have broad, efficient leaves that are too delicate to survive frost, so the trees drop them in autumn and grow more in spring. Many small plants also die back, but sprout again in spring to flower before they are shaded by the trees, like these bluebells in an English beech wood. Animal life cycles follow the plant growth, so these forests teem with life in spring but are quiet in winter.

COOL AND WET

Coastal regions with mild climates develop temperate rain forests, such as the giant redwood forests of the western United States, the bamboo forests of China, and this tree-fern forest in Tasmania, Australia. Most lie near cool oceans that keep them damp and frost-free all year round. Since the seasons are less extreme here than in deciduous forests, the plants keep growing throughout the year. They include some of the biggest trees in the world.

SCORCHED EARTH

Dry sun-baked regions have small forests of trees with leathery leaves that resist moisture loss. These include cork oak, olive, and—in Australia—eucalyptus, as eaten by this koala. The trees are adapted to survive frequent wildfires. Some even thrive on them, responding to a blaze by spreading their seeds in the scorched and cleared earth.

JUNGLE

The richest of all habitats are tropical rain forests, where daily rain fuels a dense growth of broad-leafed evergreen trees. These form an almost continuous canopy that shades the forest floor, so nonwoody plants often reach the light by growing as climbers or even taking root in the treetops. The year-round production of food supports an amazing variety of animal life including monkeys, birds, and butterflies.

MONSOON FORESTS

Some tropical regions such as India and Sri Lanka have long dry seasons. Their forests resemble tropical rain forests, but the trees lose their leaves in the dry, cool season. They are not as dense as tropical rainforests, so more light reaches the forest floor and there are more ground plants. Their animal life includes peacocks, monkeys, deer, and tigers.

Grasslands

Natural grasslands develop in regions that are too dry for forests, but not quite dry enough to be deserts. Most of them lie in the hearts of great continents, far from the ocean. There are two main types of natural grasslands—tropical savanna and temperate prairie or steppe. But many parts of the world are also covered by artificial grasslands, maintained by the intensive grazing of domestic animals such as sheep.

PLANT SURVIVOR

Grass is highly adapted to survive being eaten. Its leaves are laced with microscopic shards of glassy silica that wear down the teeth of grazing animals. Grazers have evolved ways around this, but the grass survives anyway because its leaves sprout from the base of the plant. So if they are nibbled off, it just grows more.

SAVANNA

Tropical grasslands grow in regions that are too dry for forests, and that have contrasting wet and dry seasons. The grasses grow in the rainy season and dry out when the rains stop. Some savannas have scattered trees, such as these African acacias, which are adapted to survive the drought and frequent fires. Herds of grazing animals crop the grass, and have to make long migrations in the dry season to find food.

PRAIRIE AND STEPPE

Temperate grasslands develop in dry regions with hot summers and cold winters. They are called prairies in North America, steppes in Asia, and pampas in South America. Some have scattered trees, but the driest—such as this central Asian steppe—are treeless "seas of grass."

GRAZERS AND HUNTERS

Extensive grasslands evolved in response to drier climates around 5 million years ago. This led to the evolution of specialized animals that were able to eat the abundant grass. But there is nowhere to hide on the open plains, so they also had to develop long legs and powerful muscles to escape their enemies. The hunters evolved too, giving rise to powerful predators such as this lion, seen pursuing a zebra on the African savanna.

TEEMING HORDES

The big grazing animals that live on grasslands are greatly outnumbered by smaller burrowing animals such as ground squirrels, rats, and voles, which are hunted by polecats, foxes, and hawks. There are also swarms of insects, especially ants and termites. They are preyed upon by insect-eating specialists like this South American giant anteater.

RANCHES AND FARMS

Vast areas of temperate grassland are now used as pasture for sheep and cattle. Many temperate grasslands also have deep, rich soils built up by thousands of years of grass growth, death, and decay, and so most of the prairies and the more fertile parts of the steppes have been plowed up for farmland. However, this makes the soil vulnerable to drying out and blowing away, and in places this has turned fertile grasslands into near-deserts.

BROAD PASTURES

Since grass is more likely to survive trampling and being eaten than other plants, intensive grazing tends to destroy any other vegetation and create grassland. In many parts of the world this has created broad tracts of grassland in regions where the natural vegetation would be forest. Some of these artificial grasslands have existed for many centuries, and they have evolved their own distinctive ecosystems.

Deserts

The driest regions on Earth are the deserts. They are not always hot—in fact the most extreme desert on the planet is in Antarctica, where water is locked away as ice. We normally think of deserts as hot places because many have been created by low rainfall combined with high temperatures, which make most of the moisture in the ground evaporate. But some moisture is captured by hardy plants that provide food for animals, so there is more life here than you might expect.

ARID ZONES

Deserts are defined by drought. Many, like the Sahara, have formed in the subtropics where sinking dry air stops clouds from forming. Others such as the Gobi Desert in central Asia, lie far from any ocean. The Atacama and Namib deserts are near the ocean, but get no rain because cool ocean currents make it fall over the sea. A few deserts lie in the lee of high mountain ranges that strip all the moisture from the air.

SCOURED AND CARVED

Most deserts suffer very high rates of erosion. This is because there are few plants to hold the soil together or cushion the effects of the wind or rare torrential rainstorms. Flowing water carves deep canyons and strips away any soil to expose bare rock. This is scoured by sand-loaded wind to create weird features like this isolated wind-cut rock or ventifact.

GIANT DUNES

The debris created by relentless desert erosion can form vast "sand seas" with colossal sand dunes. The sand grains blown up the windward slope of a dune drop over the crest onto the steeper leeward slope, so the sand is steadily moved downwind. So many of these dunes creep slowly across the landscape. Other dunes are less mobile, and may form long ridges aligned with the prevailing wind, or sometimes across it.

The Atacama Desert is so dry that it has been used to test equipment for detecting life on Mars.

Long roots
Desert plants must be able to survive drought. Some shrubs like this American creosote bush have very long roots to gather rainwater or reach underground supplies.

Water stores
Cacti suck up water through their roots and store it in their deeply ridged stems. As the water moves up the stem, the folds between the ridges open up to make more room.

Desert bloom
Some plants lie dormant as seeds until it rains. Then they sprout, flower, produce more seeds, and die within a few weeks, transforming the desert into a flower garden.

OASIS
This grove of palm trees in the Sahara is growing around an isolated water source known as an oasis. Oases form when the wind gouges deep troughs in low-lying areas, and exposes underground water that fell as rain long ago. In fact the water that supports these trees could be as much as 20,000 years old. One of the largest of these water supplies lies beneath the eastern Sahara; amazingly it has an estimated volume of 36,000 cubic miles (150,000 cubic kilometers).

HIDING AWAY
Small desert animals spend the hot days below ground and come out to feed at night. Food is scarce, and this gives cold-blooded animals an advantage since they need far less food than warm-blooded creatures of the same weight. Even so, many cold-blooded predators such as this scorpion are highly venomous, to ensure that when they do find prey they can kill it quickly to stop it from escaping.

DESERT NOMADS
Some large animals such as camels manage to survive in the open during the day. A camel conserves vital body moisture by not sweating until its body temperature exceeds 105°F (40.5°C). Another feature is its hump, which stores fat; this can be turned into energy and a small amount of water. The Arabian oryx—a desert antelope—has a white coat to reflect the sunlight, and a highly tuned instinct for finding shade.

Long legs are an advantage because the desert heat is fiercest at ground level. The air around a camel's body can be 77°F (25°C) cooler than the air around its feet.

Acid
A chemical that contains hydrogen that eats away alkaline substances such as limestone.

Arid
Very dry, as in a desert.

Asteroid
A relatively small, irregular rocky body orbiting the Sun.

Atmosphere
The layers of gas that surround Earth, retained by gravity.

Atmospheric pressure
The pressure created by the weight of air in the atmosphere.

Atom
The smallest particle of an element.

Bacteria
Microscopic single-celled organisms with no nucleus.

Carbohydrate
A substance such as sugar or starch that is made of carbon, hydrogen, and oxygen by a living organism such as a plant.

Cell
The smallest unit of life. It can exist as a single cell, or form part of a more complex organism.

Cell membrane
The "skin" of a cell.

Chemical reaction
A process in which the atoms of two substances are exchanged to form different substances.

Climate
The average weather of any region, and its typical weather pattern.

Colonize
To move into an area.

Comet
A body made of ice and dust that orbits the Sun.

Compound
A substance that is made of the chemically bonded atoms of two or more elements.

Condense
To change from a gas to a liquid.

Continental crust
A thick slab of relatively light rock that "floats" on the heavier rock of the Earth's mantle.

Convection currents
Circulating currents in gases or liquids, and even in hot, mobile rock, driven by temperature differences.

Crystal
A structure that may form when a liquid becomes a solid. Its shape is determined by the arrangement of its atoms.

Density
The compactness of a substance. If the substance is squeezed together, it becomes more dense.

Digest
A process by which food is broken down into simpler substances that can be absorbed by an animal's body.

Dissolve
Disperse a substance in a liquid, so completely that all its molecules are separated.

Downwind
In the direction that the wind is blowing.

Drought
A long period with no rain.

Element
A substance that is made up of just one type of atom.

Erosion
Wearing away, usually of rock, by natural forces such as flowing water, ice, or ocean waves.

Evaporate
To turn from a liquid into a gas.

Evolution
The process by which living things change over generations, forming new species. This occurs due to natural selection.

Extinct
Having died out completely. An extinct species is gone for good.

Fault
A fracture in rock strata, where one side of the fracture has moved relative to the other side.

Flash flood
A flood that rises very quickly after heavy rain, which may become a powerful torrent.

Geology
The science of rocks.

Granular
Made of grains.

Gravity
The attractive force between objects in space. The greater the mass of an object, the more gravity it has.

Grazing
Eating grass.

Greenhouse effect
The way certain gases in the atmosphere absorb heat radiated from Earth, warm up, and keep the planet warm.

Groundwater
Water that lies or flows beneath the ground surface.

Hot spot
A zone of volcanic activity caused by a stationary plume of heat beneath Earth's crust.

Igneous rock
A rock that has been formed by the cooling of molten magma or volcanic lava.

Impact energy
Energy of motion that is converted into heat.

Lava
Molten rock that erupts from a volcano.

Leeward
The side of an object that is sheltered from the wind.

Magma
Molten rock that lies within or beneath Earth's crust.

Mantle
The deep layer of hot rock that lies between Earth's crust and the core.

Mass
The same as weight, and measured in the same units, but not related to gravity; it applies in space where all objects are weightless.

Metamorphic rock
A rock that has been transformed by a geological process involving heat, intense pressure, or both.

Meteor
A fragment of space rock or ice that plunges through the atmosphere and burns up.

Meteorite
A fragment of space rock that survives its passage through the atmosphere and hits the ground.

Microbe
A microscopic living thing.

Midocean ridge
A submarine mountain chain created by volcanoes erupting through a rift in the ocean floor.

Migration
A regular movement of animals from one place to another.

Mineral
A natural solid made of one or more elements, usually with a distinctive crystal structure.

Molecule
The smallest particle of a substance that can exist without reducing it to separate elements. Each molecule is formed from atoms of those elements.

Nuclear energy
Energy released by the decay of radioactive elements, or by the fusion or splitting of atomic nuclei.

Nucleus
The central mass of something, such as an atom or a living cell.

Nutrients
Substances that living things need to build their tissues.

Oceanic crust
The relatively thin crust of solid basalt that lies above the Earth's mantle and forms the bedrock of the ocean floor.

Orbit
The path taken by a body in space that is traveling around a larger body, such as the Sun.

Organic
A substance that is derived from living things.

Organism
A living thing.

Photosynthesis
The process of using the energy of light to make sugar from carbon dioxide and water.

Planet
A large body made of rock and/or gas that orbits a star.

Plankton
The life that drifts in oceans, lakes, and other bodies of water.

Plateau
An area of relatively flat land.

Plate tectonics
The theory describing how the crust of the Earth consists of large mobile plates.

Predator
An animal that hunts and eats other live animals.

Prevailing wind
A wind that blows from a certain direction most of the time.

Prey
An animal that is killed by another animal (a predator) for food.

Protein
A complex substance that a living thing makes out of simpler chemical nutrients, and uses to build its tissues.

Radiate
To emit rays of light, heat, or other types of radiation.

Radioactive
Describes an element that is radiating energy as its atomic nuclei break down to form smaller, lighter nuclei.

Rift
A widening crack caused by rocks pulling apart.

Rift valley
A region where part of the Earth's crust has dropped into the gap formed by the crust pulling apart.

Sedimentary rock
Rock formed from compressed and hardened sediments.

Sediments
Solid particles such as sand or mud that have been transported by water, wind, ice, or gravity, and have settled in a layer.

Solar System
The system of planets, moons, and asteroids orbiting the Sun.

Solution
A liquid, usually water, containing a dissolved solid such as salt.

Star
A huge mass of hot gas in space that generates energy— including light—by nuclear fusion.

Static electricity
A buildup of electric charge.

Strata
Layers of sedimentary rock.

Stratosphere
The layer of Earth's atmosphere above the troposphere.

Subduction
A region where one tectonic plate is diving beneath another, creating an ocean trench.

Subtropics
The warm regions to the north and south of the equator that lie between the hot tropics and the cooler midlatitudes.

Superheat
To heat a liquid such as water under pressure, so it gets hotter than its normal boiling point.

Tabular
Flat, as in a table.

Tectonic plates
Plates of Earth's crust.

Temperate
A climate that is neither very hot nor very cold.

Tropics
The hot regions to the north and south of the equator, between the Tropic of Cancer and the Tropic of Capricorn.

Troposphere
The lowest layer of Earth's atmosphere.

Ultraviolet
A form of light that damages living tissue. It is invisible to humans.

Viscous
Refers to a fluid that is sticky and thick, like glue.

Vortex
A whirling motion in a fluid such as air or water, where the fluid is drawn into the center and then drawn up or down.

Water vapor
The invisible gas that forms when water molecules move apart.

Weathering
The breaking down of rocks and minerals by rain, sunlight, ice, and other climatic effects.

Windward
The side of an object that is exposed to the wind.

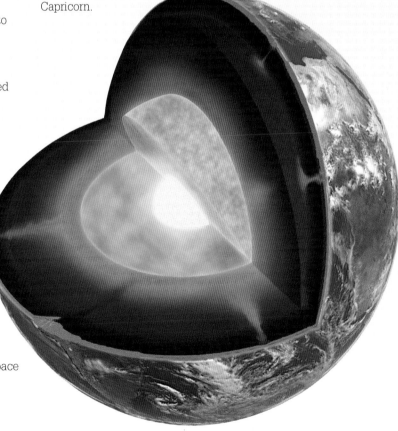

Index

A

acacia trees 64
accretion 10–11
air 13
air currents 44, 45
amber 36
ammonites 37
Andes 26–27
andesite 21
animals 55, 56–57, 65, 67
Antarctica 44, 53, 66
anteater 65
anticyclones 47
aquatic life 60–61
archaea 58–59
Arctic 44, 55
Atlantic Ocean 22, 23
atmosphere 13, 44, 58
atmospheric pressure 46–47
atoms 9, 18, 32, 33
aureoles 35
axis, Earth's 44, 54

B

bacteria 58–59, 60
basalt 20, 22, 28, 34
biodiversity 59
biosphere 57, 59
black smokers 22
bluebells 62–63
Botswana 56–57
bronze 33

C

cacti 67
calderas 29
camels 67
canyons 38, 66
carbon 58
carbon dioxide 54, 55, 59, 60
caves and caverns 40–41
cells 59
cenotes 41
chalk 35
chemical compounds 32
chemical reactions 58
cliffs 35
climate change 54–55, 61
climate zones 44–45
clouds 15, 45, 46–47, 48, 52
    supercell 49
comets 13, 14
continental drift 20
continental shelves 21
continents 19, 20–21, 23, 26, 27,
    39, 45, 54
cooling 11, 18, 58
coral reefs 41, 61
core, Earth's 12–13, 18
craters 29

crust 12–13, 18–19, 20–21
and earthquakes 24
    fold mountains 26, 39
    oceanic 20, 22
    rifts 22–23, 27, 28
crystals 32–33, 34, 41
cyanobacteria 58
cyclones 47

D

deltas 51
depressions 47
deserts 38, 45, 66–67
diamonds 33
dinosaurs 36–37, 55

E

earthquakes 13, 17, 18, 19, 23,
    24–25
ecological succession 62
ecosystems 59, 62, 65
electromagnetism 12
elements 8, 9, 10, 18, 31, 32,
    33, 58
elephants 56–57
eras, geological 20–21
erosion 27, 30–31, 38, 57, 66
    glacial 52
estuaries 51
eucalyptus 63
Europa 14
evolution 59

F

faults, geological 23, 24, 27
fish 60, 61
flatworm, marine 59
floodplains 50
food chain 60
forests 62–63
fossils 36–37
fungi 59

G

galaxies 8
gases 11, 12, 13
gemstones 33
geysers 16–17, 29

glaciers 15, 52, 54
    shrinking 55
global warming 55
gold 9, 33
granite 27, 34
grasslands 64–65
gravity 10, 12
greenhouse effect 54–55
Greenland 53

H

hailstones 48
Hawaii 28, 47
heat 18, 46
helium 8, 9
Himalayas 26, 27
hot springs 29, 58, 60
hurricanes 49
hydrogen 8, 9
hydrothermal veins 33

I

ice 14, 15, 38, 52–53
ice ages 54–55
icebergs 53
Iceland 22, 28
intrusions 35
iron oxide 32
island arcs 23
islands, volcanic 22, 23, 29

J, K

Japan 24, 25
jungles 63
Kilimanjaro, Mount 45

L

lakes 50–51, 60, 61
lava 20, 22, 23, 28, 29, 34, 39
Lesser Antilles 23
life 7, 9, 11, 17, 56–67
    aquatic 60–61
    habitats 62–67
    origins 58–59

ghtning 48
nestone 35, 40–41, 54

M

agma 29, 34, 39
antle 12, 18–19, 20, 22, 23
ars 14
eanders 51
ercury 14
etallic minerals 33
etals 12, 33
eteorites 11, 12
eteors 10
exico 41
icroclimates 47
icroraptor 36–37
id-Atlantic Ridge 22, 28
ilky Way 8
inerals 15, 31, 32–33, 34
ississippi Delta 51
olecules 58
    water 14
onsoon forests 63
onsoons 45
onument Valley 30–31
oon 10, 11, 17
ountains 18, 26–27
    climate 45
    fold mountains 26, 39
    glaciers 52–53
    ridges 22–23, 24, 28, 47

N

tural selection 59
eutrons 18
omads 67
orth Pole 44, 53
    magnetic 12
uclear energy 18
uclear fusion 8, 9, 31

O

ases 67
ceans 14–15, 20–21, 45, 58
    currents 54
    floors 20, 22–23
    life 60–61

polar 53
    rifts and trenches 22–23
orbital cycles 54
ores 33
organisms 58–59
oxbow lakes 51
oxygen 58, 61
ozone 13, 58

P, Q

Pacific Plate 19, 23
Pacific ring of fire 19
pampas 64
particles 18
peridotite 20
photosynthesis 9, 58, 60, 61, 62
phytoplankton 60
pillow lavas 20
planets 8–9
    formation 10–11
plankton 60
plants 9, 59, 62
    desert 67
plates, tectonic 18–19, 20,
    22–23, 24–25, 26, 28
polar bears 55
polar regions 44, 45, 47, 52–53
ponds 61
prairies 64–65
proteins 58
protons 9, 18
quartz 33

R

radioactive decay 18
rain 15, 40, 45, 46–47, 48
rain forests 63
Richter Scale 24–25
ridges 22–23, 24, 28, 47
rifts 22–23, 27, 28
rivers 50–51
    life 60, 61
    underground 40
rock cycle 31, 38–39, 50, 57
rocks 12, 18, 20, 21, 31,
    34–41, 57
    carbonate 54
    crumple zones 27

igneous 34, 38
intrusions and aureoles 35
metamorphic 35, 38, 39
minerals in 31, 32–33, 34
sedimentary 34, 35, 38, 39
strata 27, 34
volcanic 20, 27
rust 32

S

Sahara Desert 54, 66, 67
salt 9, 32, 33
San Andreas Fault 23
sand 38
sand dunes 66
Santorini 29
savanna 64
scorpions 67
seas, coastal 21
seasons 44, 54
sediments 34, 38, 39, 50
seismology 13, 25
sinkholes 40
snow 52–53
"Snowball Earth" 55
solar energy 44, 46, 54, 58
Solar System 8–9
stalactites and stalagmites 41
stars 8–9
steppe 64–65
storms 48–49
stratovolcanoes 28–29
streams 50, 51, 61
stromatolites 58
sugar 58, 59, 60
Sun 8–9, 14, 44, 46, 48, 54
supercell clouds 49
supernovas 9
swallow holes 40

T

taiga 62
temperate regions 47, 63, 64–65
thunder 48
tornadoes 42–43, 49
trees 62–63, 64, 67
trenches, ocean 22–23, 24
tropics 44, 45, 47, 61, 63, 64

tsunamis 25
tube worms 60

U, V, W

Universe 7
uranium 18
valleys
    glacial 52–53, 54
    networks 50
    rift 27
viperfish 60
volcanic islands 22, 23, 29
volcanoes 12, 17, 18, 23, 28–29
    and basalt 20
    and climate change 55
    magma 29, 34, 39
    Pacific region 19
    undersea 20, 21
    and water vapor 13
water 9, 11, 13, 14–15, 40
    in the desert 66, 67
    and life 60–61
water cycle 15
water vapor 14–15, 46, 47
waterfalls 40, 50
weather 15, 42, 44–47
    extreme 48–49
wetlands 50–51, 56–57
wildfires 63
winds 46–47, 66, 67
    prevailing 45, 47

Z

zooplankton 60

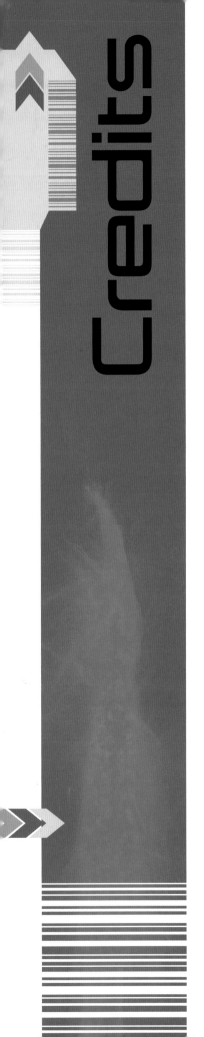

Credits

Dorling Kindersley would like to thank Katie Knutton for additional artworks, Charlotte Webb for proofreading, John Searcy for Americanization, and Jackie Brind for the index.

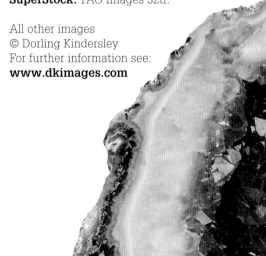